OUR VIRTUOUS REPUBLIC

THE FORGOTTEN CLAUSE IN THE AMERICAN SOCIAL CONTRACT

RICHARD D. BARIS

DEDICATION

The efforts made in working on this book would never have made it onto paper if it weren't for the support of my father, uncle, my mother-in-law, and most of all – my wife. There is a certain solace that one seeks out in times of doubt and despair, which can only be found within the strength of their family. The unconditional love and support they offered to me in one such time reminded me of something I had long forgotten. The virtuous obligation of one to their family, community, the desire of a son to instill pride in their parents, and the duty of a man to be deserving of their wife's love; these are the strongest of human motivations, and the only source of honest success. In addition to my children, this book is for all of you. I hope you all consider it a validation and manifestation of your wisdom…for believing in me. I love you all.

- Rich

CONTENTS

PREFACE   i

1   THE FORGOTTEN CLAUSE   1

    INTRODUCTION   1

    A SICK PATIENT ON TOXIC MEDICINE   12

    THE PSYCHOLOGY OF VIRTUE   15

    INDIVIDUAL CITIZENSHIP, OBLIGATION TO COMMUNITY, & THE STATE OF OUR UNION   32

2   PROGRESS OVER VIRTUE   43

    THE CONTRACT IS BROKEN   43

    THE BIRTH OF BIG GOVERNMENT CRONYISM & DEMOCRATIC DESPOTISM   52

    THE INVENTION OF RETIREMENT & THE MANUFACTURED CRISIS   66

    THE REST IS HISTORY   78

3   VIRTUE IN SOCIETY   87

    THE DECAPITATION OF CHURCH & STATE   87

    FAMILY DECOMPOSITION   106

    POVERTY, THE ETHIC, & THE HIERARCHY OF NEEDS   110

    THE EDUCATION VACCINATION: INOCULATING AGAINST RATIONAL IGNORANCE   117

    TARGETING EMPOWERMENT & THE RIGHT OF PROTECTION   126

4   THE CHOICE   131

    HONESTY IS THE BEST POLICY   131

    THE NATURE OF GOVERNMENT   132

    CONCLUSION   134

PREFACE

As an adolescent, and even a young adult, my father used to tell me that I would not be the first person in history to successfully uproot the natural order, or something of that nature. However, it was not until I was in adulthood with life experience did I come to understand what he meant by order. As an unruly youth, which in many ways I still am, I assumed he was referring to government order, the schools, or the police. Despite the warnings nothing seemed to stop me from trying, and nothing seemed to be of consequence from my efforts. However, my father was not referencing a superficial order, and indeed, there were consequences to come. Yet, we learn the most valuable lessons in truth from consequence, it reveals to us what does exist but cannot be seen. I was fortunate to suffer in a sense, as I never would have learned certain truths without painful experience.

Past indiscretions had threatened to condemn me to a life of two different manmade prisons. First, in the traditional sense of incarceration, and second, to the structural prison that progressive government has created disguised as public service. I observed that returning to the traditional principles of self-reliance, personal responsibility, duty and faith, equipped me with the tools I needed to regain control of my own destiny. America has been and must remain, a country of citizens who plot a course to achieve their dreams, and are willing to work hard to realize those dreams. Pursuing higher education in my late twenties provided me a unique perspective for which my younger classmates were not privy. My approach to academics was one from a real world mindset. Thus, when undergraduate studies requires and over emphasis on Marx while Weber is met with silence in the same manner as a bad joke, it is obvious where the majority of our problems are coming from. However, that is only half of the story.

Our society must have opportunity that maximizes mobility for all, and I do mean all, who are invested and believe in their dream. No longer can our society turn away those who earn and deserve a second chance, while promoting idleness that inevitably leads to mischief and reliance. There is an overwhelming sentiment among the American people that the system is rigged against us. Much of this is of course due to the divisive rhetoric of our leaders hoping to appeal to these public perceptions. Political expediency has taken precedent over the difficult decisions we expect leaders to have the courage to make. Sometimes real leadership requires you admit you don't have all of the answers. Let us begin this discussion of problems, which only *We the People* have the power to solve.

CHAPTER 1: THE FORGOTTEN CLAUSE

"Only a virtuous people are capable of freedom. As nations become corrupt and vicious, they have more need of masters."[1]

Benjamin Franklin

INTRODUCTION

This book is not meant for historians. As did the father of our Constitution, James Madison, I revere history and recognize that it offers a rare opportunity to understand human behavior. Political, economical, and socio-cultural studies help us to discover the truth of human nature because it manifests in the form of historical reoccurrences. In human civilization, certain behavioral patterns are constant regardless of region, race, or era. The aim of this book is not to provide Americans with a history lesson, but to use history to reintroduce Americans to themselves. Unfortunately, in our society there are those who believe history proves a most useful tool when manipulated to support a false narrative, or rather an alternate reality. They have charged entire education and media institutions with the responsibility to keep the truth of our history where they believe it belongs – in the past.

This book is not meant for political scholars. The domination of academic institutions by the progressive left too often prevents an honest discussion of political issues. It is counterproductive to argue against out of context positions from within a cage of political correctness, which of course was purposefully constructed to control the debate. Many modern scholars are resolved to have their profession be that of myth-maker. They have distorted the beliefs, intentions and characters, of many prominent historical figures in our shared American past. These institutions have betrayed the very public that entrusted them with the sacred duty to educate our children. Nevertheless, I intend to use the same scholastic method that breathes life into their abstract and impractical arguments to debunk them as the bias they are. Incompetent and under qualified politicians repeatedly adopt proposals predicated upon their ideas, which ultimately prove to be policies unfit for real world implementation. These failures, at best, are a waste money and at worst, do more damage to society than if there had been no action taken at all. Either way, our society is no better for their efforts.

This book is meant for the American people; by which, I refer not only to those who may currently share my political persuasion, but also to the union worker or teacher; the young women whose decision may or may not have given

---

[1] Franklin, Benjamin. *The Writings of Benjamin Franklin*. Edited by Albert Henry Smyth. Vol. 9 pg. 569 New York: The Macmillan Co., 1905 – 1907

her the highest of blessings, but also nature's greatest responsibility; the unemployed father receiving assistance to feed his family, or the single-mother who is feeling isolated and alone; the immigrant who feels unfamiliar and displaced; and of course, all others who strive to possess that rare commodity we call truth. Truth, itself, has become a commodity in our society, as the efforts of a few to conceal truth have proven quite effective. It is often said that "patience is a virtue." The act of patience itself, however, is not always motivated by virtuous intentions. To the credit of the competent action and strong resolve of the "artificial aristocracy," the people of America have lost their national identity.[2] We suffer from a national collective amnesia as a result of deliberate measures taken by patient despots. In a free society, citizens must become masters of their own historical record. Every generation that passes ignorant of this task grows closer to the dangers of despotism. "The Great Communicator," President Ronald Reagan, is widely remembered for his speech in which he said:

"Freedom is never more than one generation away from extinction. We didn't pass it on to our children in the bloodstream. It must be fought for, protected, and handed on for them to do the same, or one day we will spend our sunset years telling our children and our children's children what it was once like in the United States where men were free."[3]

The paramount problem with conservatives and the country as a whole, is that we have forgotten how to fight for, protect, and hand freedom off to our children. Issues and ideas are now almost exclusively fought on policy platforms, which of course is the realm of government, and politicians have a monopoly on these matters. Historical truths get lost in the government debate trap, and in what many Americans believe to be our "sunset years" we debate absolute truth against relativism. It is my deepest desire to remind the American people that there is in fact an absolute truth, and they have no need to consult the pretentious wisdom of our leadership any longer. They are not what they purport to be, that is, our salvation in time of need and crisis. Government has no intention to rescue us, nor would they even know how, from the many malevolent forces that scheme against the people. In fact, they are those forces and tirelessly work to conceal their intentions. Time and time again, we have allowed out of our own convenience to let them convince us that their station can provide us with the solutions our society needs. *We the People* possess all that is needed to restore and preserve our way of life for our "children and our children's children."

More than any other nation in history, the United States has made itself the new home for immigrants in search of a better life. Mass migrations brought people of various origins to the shores of America, often with little or nothing

---

[2] Reference to Jefferson's name for leaders who have assumed power not from talent and virtue, but from birth, wealth, and relations. They prevent any others rise to equal station.
[3] President Ronald Reagan's speech to the Phoenix Chamber of Commerce. March 30th, 1961

more than their work ethic, willing to do something rarely seen in such large numbers; abandon native nationalism and adopt the American identity. International relations realist Kenneth Waltz, correctly argued that nationalism is more powerful than ideology.[4] Nationalism, or the "nation," has proven difficult to define. Marxist academics have spent more than a century developing arguments to disprove what has seemed to be real, yet could not be seen. Tom Nairn, who is often referred to as the heir to the Marxist school of social science, painfully but courageously remarked:

"The theory of nationalism represents Marxism's great historical failure."[5]

The implication from this is that some elements to our original American social contract, deep in the human psyche, are understood to be truths more than manmade ideas. Perhaps, they are even natural? The unique place America holds in history is the uniting of diverse cultures and people behind a single national identity; the irony of how the dominant capitalist nation accomplished what Marxism could not was never lost on Nairn. Those who came to make a new life in America were seeking out a place in a society where free people were empowered with the right to their own talents and labor, which gave them the opportunity to grow and exist in a state of happiness. Emma Lazarus famously captured this sentiment in her sonnet which read:

> *"'Keep, ancient lands, your storied pomp!' cries she*
> *With silent lips. 'Give me your tired, your poor,*
> *Your huddled masses yearning to breathe free,*
> *The wretched refuse of your teeming shore.'"[6]*

Long before ink ever touched the paper that would be stained with those immortal words, the "tired," the "poor," the "huddled masses yearning to breathe free," were producing American prosperity at a pace the world had never before seen. The European existence could not accomplish the same promise. It seems evident that prior explanations have proven superficial at best. What can account for such a transformation in human potential among these people? Free to pursue the desire in our hearts through the reason in our minds, we vindicated the American experiment, along with those who were thought foolish enough to dream of such an idealistic possibility. History and the world bore witness to the innovations of the free mind; the likes of which, were powerful enough to thrust humanity out of the world's natural darkness and into the artificial light. In

[4] Walt, Kenneth. *Man, the State, & War: a theoretical analysis.* pg. 124 – 157 Columbia University Press 1954
[5] Nairn, Tom. *The Break-up of Britain.* pg. 329 London: New Left Books, 1977
[6] Lazarus, Emma. *The New Colossus*, 1883. Library of Congress

essence, they pursued existence in a society where the relationship between the individual citizen and the State was tailored to the unique characteristics of human nature. In America, we were and are unique, in the sense that we called that existence "citizenship."

At the heart of our American social contract are our founding documents. The genius of their construction lay ironically on both a contradiction, and a consistency. The Declaration of Independence and our Constitution profess the same belief in certain truths with an aim toward the same end, but the manner in which those beliefs are conveyed differ. The former, or the Declaration, is a wholly idealistic document demanding equality, liberty, and property. The latter represents the very present element of realism in the Age of Enlightenment, specifically in the Bill of Rights, which acknowledges the precautions that must be taken to protect those ideals. The colonies juxtaposed to Europe were idealistic to be sure, but Natural Law was viewed as a real world observation of human limitations, as well as the precautions necessary to maintain order and liberty. The Constitution is a document that was deliberated upon by men with no delusions about the darker aspects to human nature. The framers sought to apply a form of government that would encourage the best of human behavior, while discouraging and safeguarding against the worst. As a testament to the wisdom of their beliefs, America has contributed more to the productive advancement of the human race than any other civilization. However, for all of the mechanisms put in place by the Constitution, liberty is still conditional upon the amount of civic obligation the people feel to protect it.

I am not of the persuasion, as some other conservative thinkers are, to deify or elevate our Founding Fathers to an almost demigod status. Failing to acknowledge and accept the imperfections of their humanity minimizes their accomplishments, and makes it more difficult for us to defend them against their critics. These were men that felt human emotions the same as we. They struggled to comprehend the events of their time as we do today, but they did so with a comprehensive worldview that was "unique in its moral and intellectual appeal."[7] These are qualities, which of course, we are sorely lacking in our own understanding of the world we live in. Americans, now, are all or nothing in there approach to decision-making; whereas, our Founding Fathers were hungry "all over" for the truth, and would approach problem solving from several different dimension in an effort to at least stay true to truth.[8] The Founding Fathers relied on many intellectual authorities, of which none of them alone save Locke claim clear dominance. English common law, specifically Sir Edward Coke, had clear influence on the Founding Fathers and served to legitimize a

---

[7] Bailyn, Bernard. *The Ideological Origins of the American Revolution.* pg. 22 Cambridge, MA: Belknap of Harvard University Press, 1992

[8] Reference used by psychologist Abraham Maslow to describe intensity in which humans pursue the goals that are deemed by human nature necessary.

position; however, such is the nature of manmade laws, each interpreted the common law in their own respect. Philosophers of the Enlightenment such as Rousseau, Montesquieu, and especially Locke, were authorities on Natural Law and served during the Revolution to justify defiance of the unjust laws of politicians. Long before Locke, Natural Law had been observed in Roman antiquity by Cicero, Plutarch and Tacitus, "writers who had lived either when the republic was being fundamentally challenged or when its greatest days were already past and its moral and political virtues had decayed."[9] In much the same fashion that some do today, the Founding Fathers despised the social and political trends in Europe, which they compared to the latter years of the Roman republic, when the virtue, patriotism, liberty and justice, all had waned from civil society. What further emerges from the colonial literature as a source of political and social theory is New England Puritanism, which throughout the 18th century would converge all other religious enlightenment thinking into the American mainstream Protestant ethic. The coalescing of these philosophies seem in many ways a contradiction, as the Anglo-American crisis intensified the tenets of Natural Law justified independence, yet the common law appealed to the lack of precedent and to the unbroken tradition of the social contract. Natural Law and Protestantism reconciled in God the manner in which reverence for the tradition of common law could be preserved, while at the same time cast off its restrictions that have burdened the Spirit in the past. The common law, after all, is a worldly law and through no fault of the system came our inability to improve our state of being.

Ultimately, the signing of the Declaration of Independence represented a break from the Hobbesian interpretation of the social contract that dominated Europe for generations, and in many ways still does. England had experienced revolution in the sense that the monarchy now shared power in a limited constitutional monarchy, but they were subjects nonetheless. The relationship between a king and his subjects, which for us may be impossible to fully comprehend, was one comparable to a father-son. This relationship was absolute, that is to say, a subject could no more dissolve his ties with the monarch than a son could disown his father. In *Leviathan*, Hobbes describes the reigning interpretation of the British social contract:

"And he that carrieth this person, is called SOVEREIGN, and said to have sovereign power, and every one besides, his SUBJECT. The attaining to this sovereign power, is by two ways. One, by natural force; as when a man maketh his children, to submit themselves, and their children, to his government, as being able to destroy them if they refuse; or by war subdueth

---

[9] Bailyn, Bernard. *The Ideological Origins of the American Revolution*. pg. 25 Cambridge, MA: Belknap of Harvard University Press, 1992

his enemies to his will, giving them their lives on that condition.[10]

Although Englishmen were said to be free, the dynastic authority who were supposedly entrusted by God were also obliged to protect and provide them with freedom as a father protects his child. By declaring independence from King George III, the Founders asserted that men were naturally free and political society, or the original social contract predated dynastic authority. Therefore, as John Locke contended, rights were God-given and sovereignty invariably rests with the people. In *Two Treatises of Government*, Locke argues republican sovereignty:

"But to conclude, Reason being plain on our side, that Men are naturally free, and the Examples of History shewing, that the Governments of the World, that were begun in Peace, had their beginning laid on that foundation, and were made by the Consent of the People; There can be little room for doubt, either where the Right is, or what has been the Opinion, or Practice of Mankind, about the first erecting of Governments."[11]

Locke was a proponent of a breakable social contract, which was unheard of in political practice at the time. The actions of our Founders were an affirmation of Lockean philosophy, which again, had no real world precedent. Independence, however, was far from certain in the minds of the Founding Fathers. Indeed, unlike the modern portrayal of inevitability, it remained the least desirable outcome to many of our Founders. Even at the height of English oppression, there remained the sentiment among the American colonists of deep affection and connection to the motherland. Admiration for England fed the persisting inclination to remain British subjects, comfortable and secure in what Franklin referred to as "that fine and noble China vase."[12]

Prior to King George's proclamation in 1775 that America was in rebellion, which was tantamount to a declaration of war, the colonial delegates incessantly pleaded for his protection from the tyrants in Parliament. In *Letters of Novanglus*, Johns Adams made a painstaking effort to clarify his position, which was one of apprehension regarding independence.[13] Published in 1775, he joined colonial attacks against the authority of Parliament, but favored a commonwealth of states throughout the British empire. The commonwealth of states, an idea that was

[10] Hobbes, Thomas. *Leviathan.* Ch. XVII pg. 339 – 340, *Of the Causes, Generation, and Definition of a Commonwealth, 1651.* Edited by Frederick J.E. Woodbridge. New York: Charles Scribner's Sons, 1958

[11] Locke, John. *Two Treatises of Government.* Edited by Peter Laslett. pg. 380 New York: Mentor Books, 1963

[12] Quoted from Middlekauff, Robert. *The Glorious Cause: The American Revolution, 1763 – 1789* Revised & Expanded Edition. pg. 686 Oxford University Press 2005

[13] *The Letters of Novanglus, 1775. Papers of John Adams.* Edited by Robert Joseph Taylor. Vol. 2. Cambridge, MA: Belknap of Harvard University Press, 1977

quite common, granted colonial legislatures sovereignty and put them on equal ground with Parliament. However, Adams was a great admirer of the English common law, and found in the law little precedent for subject departure out from under the British crown.

On the other hand, Thomas Jefferson bypassed manmade law altogether in his arguments against English rule. The law of England was subject to measurement against the "Laws of Nature and Nature's God." Ultimately, the agreement between Natural Law and the Protestant worldview undeniably provided a moral justification for independence. After all, if the monarch was ordained by God, then who would be more diligent than he to oblige Him. In 1774, just before the proclamation was issued, Jefferson petitioned the king for redress:

"...an humble and dutiful address be presented to his majesty, begging leave to lay before him, as chief magistrate of the British empire, the united complaints of his majesty's subjects in America; complaints which are excited by many unwarranted encroachments and usurpations, attempted to be made by the legislature of one part of the empire, upon those rights which God and the laws have given equally and independently to all."[14]

The social contract was between the monarch and his subjects, and therefore, appeared to the colonists as a reasonable resolution. Alas, none would receive a response. They felt betrayal the same as we, stemming from their fellow Englishmen's inability to reject immoralities and corruption in order to secure their countrymen's freedom. It wasn't only British oppression that was feared, but the possibility that British immorality had begun to infect American virtue:

"By 1776 it had become increasingly evident that if they were to remain the kind of people they wanted to be they must become free of Britain. The calls for independence thus took on a tone of imperativeness...Only separating from the British monarch and instituting republicanism, it seemed, could realize the social image the Enlightenment had drawn of them."[15]

The Continental Congress convened in the wake of the king's proclamation, which brought the debate surrounding the king's obligation to a close and persuaded the colonists to accept the disagreements that prevailed against separation, moving opinion rapidly in favor of independence.[16] This will be discussed further in chapter 3, but the Founding Fathers had soon developed the

---

[14] Jefferson. Thomas. *Thomas Jefferson Asserts American Rights, 1774.* pg. 257 – 258 *A Summary View of the Rights of British America.* Williamsburg, 1774

[15] Wood, Gordon S. *The Creation of the American Republic, 1776 – 1787.* pg. 108 Chapel Hill NC: University of North Carolina Press, 1969

[16] Brown, Richard D. *Major Problems in the Era of the American Revolution, 1760-1791: Documents and Essays.* pg. 139 2nd Edition. Lexington, Mass: D.C. Heath, 2000

realization that God had placed them in a unique position in history to redeem humankind. For their acts of virtue it was viewed that they were on the right side of God's will and law, thus justified in their action. Washington, Madison, Franklin and Adams, all would look back at the Revolution and the adoption of the Constitution and see the assistance of divine providence. Yet still, colonial American political discourse was ripe with argument and disagreement. The spirit of cooperation between 1776 – 1787, was short lived and quickly gave way to quarrel; but that does not justify the recent lack of deference for their wisdom. The establishment of a free society despite all of the flaws, which have failed humankind in our past, is what made them truly exceptional.

Progressives have sought to overly humanize our Founding Fathers in an effort to focus new generations on their failings. That will never be sufficient to negate the fact that in approximately five thousand years of human civilization, never had there existed a nation of free, self-governed people before the United States. The globalist view, which seeks to denounce or disprove American exceptionalism, will forever struggle to reconcile these truths. The demise of nationalism long prophesized by globalists and their academic allies, as one prominent scholar of nationalism has put it, "is not remotely in sight."[17] The overwhelming majority of extraordinary developments in human history, which occurred throughout the 19th and 20th centuries were American productions. The American mainstream Protestant ethic and code of traditional values proved more productive and prosperous than our European counterparts, as their wealth in social and political institutions would soon be bankrupt.

Progressives often advocate the idea of societal inclusiveness without distinguishing between national culture and national identity. The two are not one in the same as they intentionally portray them to be. American culture has always been a dynamic fusion of nationalities each boasting their own proud contribution. The American identity is one in which a static set of ideas prevails with the purpose to fulfill the promise of life, liberty, and property. These are the promises of our American social contract, and they were born out of Natural Law and the Protestant ethic, which dominate the image of our national identity. The philosophy of hard work, civic duty, social and economic mobility, indeed all that constitutes the "American dream," are foundational tenets of the Protestant ethic. Although an understanding of such an idea was widely propagated among earlier generations of Americans, increased secularization has diluted the modern American consciousness. As a result, educating the whole of the public on the consequences of removing this ethic have diminished. In his examination on the origins of capitalism, Max Weber found both the origin of capitalism and America's national identity lay in the same space, but condemned the failure of its recognition:

[17] Anderson, Benedict. *Imagined Communities*. pg. 3 New Edition. New York: Verso, 2006

"The modern man is in general, even with the best will, unable to give religious ideas a significance for culture and national character which they deserve."[18]

Weber had his own secular academic opposition to contend with, which the various Marxist scholars of Europe had sorely underestimated, but his vindicated thesis should be on display to serve as a dire warning to those who foolishly seek to "fundamentally transform" the American identity. Rousseau described the properties of the social contract as a set of clauses that are unspoken, existent and delicate. The American national identity is unlike any other in that it was codified at the beginning of our entering into a social contract. Inside the words of the law can be found a deep belief in the ethic, and a promise of a higher state of existence for those who obey it. However, there can be no expectation for either party to abide by the terms of a contract if the other is found to be in breach or default. Rousseau was correct to claim:

"The clauses of this social contract are so determined by the nature of the act that the slightest modifications would make them vain and ineffective, . . ."[19]

A great deal of effort has been put into the study of the growth of government. Progressive politicians and academics have faulted market failures, or economic crisis, for the rapid expansion of government throughout the past century. They have attempted to make the argument that the American economic system, absent government intervention has failed to provide citizens with equal opportunity and prosperity. Government must play a role in the market and other aspects of private life to ensure that opportunity is "fair." Not only has this explanation been inadequate and inaccurate, but is more a justification for the growth of government than an actual explanation. In *Crisis and Leviathan* for instance, arguably the single-most effective counterargument, Robert Higgs demonstrates that government growth occurs for a number of reasons that economics cannot account for.[20] Individuals, ideology, historical events, and so on, have all contributed to "Big Government" in a manner which narrow economic models cannot account. Orthodox fields of study in politics, however, largely ignore cultural, philosophical and psychological changes, that have occurred within American society; and almost never save for Higgs, are those transformations by despotic design. Certainly there remains the question:

---

[18] Weber, Max. *The Protestant Ethic and Spirit of Capitalism.* pg. 125 New York: Rutledge Publishing, 1992

[19] Rousseau, Jean-Jacques. *The Social Contract.* Ch. VI pg. 190 C.D.H. Cole. London: J.M. Dent 1993

[20] Higgs, Robert. *Crisis and Leviathan: Critical Episodes in the Growth of American Government.* New York: Oxford University Press, 1987

Why do we permit government to play such a role, especially in areas of our private life which previously the American psyche would have thought unacceptable and unthinkable? Prior to the Progressive Era, government was viewed with deep suspicion and thought of only as a last resort. In modern America, not only have we become complacent to intrusion, many of us rely on government for our basic needs, and even more puzzling, whole groups of activists expect government to protect individual rights and promote equal opportunity. This displays a fundamental misunderstanding of the nature of government. The only sufficient explanation for such a dramatic shift would have to account for why it is that our citizens' needs are so vast, and what about society prevents us from addressing them ourselves. In this dialogue, I am greatly concerned how government's role to fulfill these needs have affected our social contract, and what psychological effects might those "modifications" have on our behavior and happiness to the detriment of political prosperity?

An exercise in national introspection, of which I can guarantee a healthy degree of pain will be derived, is necessary if we hope to answer these questions. Salvaging our social contract and our way of life for future generations will depend upon us answering them. We will examine the relationship between the citizen and the State in the context of current political and cultural issues, such as government assistance, debt, taxes, religion, poverty and violence. Through an honest assessment of our national condition and how we arrived at this present state, we can be free to start a discussion that will plot the steps we need to take to solve the enormous challenges that lay ahead. But first, we must have an understanding of our founding ideals, their origins, evolution, reasoning and subsequent distortion. The fundamentals have been lost and with them, our understanding of how to rediscover our unique American identity. Our identity doesn't simply encompass who we are and who we want to be, but our system of government was designed to accommodate its characteristics; which of course, is exactly why it is under assault. Charting that path forward, both intellectually and in practice, requires us all to understand what it really means to be a citizen under our Constitution.

There is a forgotten clause within the American social contract, which *We the People* have violated. The Constitution's promise to protect our natural rights through limited government, is and always was, conditional upon us upholding our oath to the Constitution and fulfilling our civic obligations. Proponents of government are forever searching for, and forever creating, weaknesses in civil society for which they can propose more government purpose. Social instigations and challenges to traditionalism have no doubt proven consequential to civil society, as increased public dependency on government is symptomatic of our society defaulting on our obligations to ourselves and each other. Whether for basic needs or personal safety, citizen dependency on government must be the responsibility of our civil society to limit. The less we can depend upon each other, then the more our citizens must depend on government to subsidize our deficiencies. Our Founding Fathers understood that a citizen's willingness to sacrifice their selfishness for the well-being of the community – "such patriotism or love of country – the eighteenth century termed public virtue."[21] Civic duty, or obligation to one's community, is the source of strength for civil institutions and can only be realized through virtue. Virtue, both public and private, for the purpose of this discussion could appropriately be understood as a personal and professional ethic; from which, behavior in accordance with the laws of morality and duty are developed and sustained.

There is a vast territory between the individual and the State, which provides both a physical and psychological barrier of protection – the community. As is the case with any other territory, it must rely on willing and capable individuals to defend its borders. The most effective defense is an impenetrable civil society that renders government "unnecessary and improper" by meeting their civil obligations. The relationship between virtue and liberty is proportional, and as such, we must constantly strive for their equilibrium. As societies' virtue wanes, so too does the strength of civil society, thus progressive government grows at the natural expense to our liberty. The balance has shifted heavily in favor of tyranny. Our national condition is grave yet self-inflicted, and is but a symptom of a disease from which our society suffers - insufficient virtue. There is a price we must pay for government to provide to our citizens that which we should be providing ourselves, and that price is our freedom. Social services, at least for now, have become essential to some extent; therefore, the only questions that remain are who will provide them, and who has the natural capacity to render them unnecessary in the future.

Progressive policies have a negative impact not only on personal freedom, economic prosperity and political discourse, but our national psychology, as well. The idea that we can defer to government-centered solutions while remaining a free society is both patently false, as well as an intentional obfuscation pushed by progressives in both major political parties. Their foolish allies in academia plant in society a false sense of security in government, it is reinforced through popular culture, and reaffirmed in the state-run media. Within our government there is, always was and always will be, political players bent on expanding their influence and limiting the rights of the people. Whether the end result is revealed to be socialism or fascism, either of which could be argued, America has been on a slow but steady march to the tyranny of totalitarianism by popular support. Recently, this pace has begun to accelerate. *We the People* must make a decision whether to re-take responsibility by re-establishing the balance between our rights and obligations, or accept a new social contract that guarantees neither freedom, nor prosperity. If we fail, indeed, "one day we will spend our sunset

---

[21] Wood, Gordon S. *The Creation of the American Republic, 1776 – 1787.* pg. 68 Chapel Hill NC: University of North Carolina Press, 1969

years telling our children and our children's children what it was once like in the United States where men were free."[22]

For all of the discussion concerning original intent, it is surprising that we have come to rely so heavily upon the document itself, while dismissing our own burden of responsibility. Samuel Adams wrote of the burden we were originally intended to bear, the burden we have ignored for far too long:

"The sum of all is, if we would most truly enjoy the gift of Heaven [freedom], let us become a virtuous people; then shall we both deserve and enjoy it. While, on the other hand, if we are universally vicious and debauched in our manners, though the form of our Constitution carries the face of the most exalted freedom, we shall in reality be the most abject slaves."[23]

A SICK PATIENT ON TOXIC MEDICINE

Despite any presumptions one might entertain, and indeed Americans presume in excess, I am not in agreement with prior conservative arguments. The progressive ideology exacerbates cultural deficiencies and perpetuates political problems, but it alone is not the cause of either. Despotism is as old as human civilization itself. Progressivism is merely the philosophical form of its latest natural evolution, a popular tyranny which promises "civil disorder and the early assumption of power by a dictator;" tailored to appeal to peoples in Western free countries.[24] Upon studying, in total, the happenings of the Progressive Era, I cannot help but to be reminded of the commonly practiced process of re-gifting. The similarities are really quite striking, that is to say, it is the despotic junk from history rejected by our Founding Fathers, which has been put in a new box, wrapped in shinier paper, and given to a later, unknowing recipient at a future time. In this case, the unknowing recipient is a future generation ignorant of the dangers, tactics, rhetoric and historical truths. Although, this form is not new either; in fact, progressive tactics mirror the same despotic tactics used in Rome during the time of Marcus Tullius Cicero. He, too, lived in an era in which society was moving toward tyranny by popular support.[25] Statesmen in the Roman Senate were corrupt, complacent, afraid, or simply agreed with Caesar. The masses, it was believed by the Senators, were too easy to exploit not to exploit them. Our Founding Fathers admired Cicero, especially

---

[22] President Ronald Reagan's speech to the Phoenix Chamber of Commerce. March 30th, 1961

[23] Adams. Samuel. Quoted from Wells, William V. *The Life and Public Services of Samuel Adams.* Vol. 1 pg. 22 – 23 Boston: Little, Brown and Company, 1865

[24] Bailyn, Bernard. *The Ideological Origins of the American Revolution.* pg. 282 Cambridge, MA: Belknap of Harvard University Press, 1992

[25] Ebenstein, William. *Great Political Thinkers.* pg. 122 – 123 New York: Holt, Rinehart and Winston, 1963

James Madison, and they envisioned a nation where:

"True law is right reason in agreement nature; it is of universal applications, unchanging and everlasting; it summons to duty by its commands, and averts from wrongdoing by its prohibitions."[26]

Conservatives, however, have been just as complacent in the failure to observe humankind's "unchanging and everlasting" laws. Unfortunately, in failing to observe the Natural Law we fail to answer when "it summons to duty by its commands." Our constitutional government was predicated upon duties for both citizens and leaders, neither of which are sufficiently being carried out. Before we dive into the burden of scholastic argument to make "self-evident" my claim, let us first entertain the fun of metaphor. To better illustrate my argument I have likened our political discourse to a sick patient.

Let's pretend there is a patient whom we will call "Patient Citizen." He suffers from many serious symptoms, including amnesia. He is under the care of the attending physician Doctor Left, and his ever-ambitious colleague, Doctor Right. Doctor Left has deliberately managed the symptoms with treatments that have worsened his patient's condition. He has concluded that as long as he keeps the patient comfortable and quiet, then he remains the attending physician. Both have ignored the root cause of the disease, albeit for different reasons.

The ever-ambitious Doctor Right, would love to be the new attending physician at the hospital. However, he must attempt a treatment that improves the condition of the patient. He would have to give the patient medicine that will cause him great discomfort – the truth serum. He fears that he has allowed this self-perpetuating disease to go on for so long, that if he was to give the patient the truth serum now, the patient will erupt in dangerous behavior and he will be held responsible as well. His compliance was a result of his own ambition and is equally shameful.

The truth, is that "Patient Citizen" has amnesia and has forgotten that he doesn't even need a doctor. The not-so well-meaning doctors had convinced him to come into the hospital, because they were *concerned* he could not properly look out for his own health. The drugs prescribed to keep him comfortable, intentionally prolong the amnesia, are highly addictive, cause atrophy and will soon run out. A once healthy and productive individual, has been made into a hypochondriac who now fears that every little sniffle will require medical attention.

That is a dilemma for the doctors who swore to do what is best for their patient. Even if they had the wisdom to find one, at this point administering a cure is not in their best interest. Despite the fact "Patient Citizen" has zero

---

[26] Ibid. pg. 133

quality of life and an even worse prognosis, the nature of their position requires an awakening from the patient in order for them to change the treatment. "Patient Citizen" can no longer rely on his doctors and must take responsibility for his own health if he truly wants to get well and live again. The atrophy ensures a painful recovery, and he must endure much needed physical therapy before his quality of life improves to the point he self-validates his decision. But ultimately, until he finds the courage to check himself out of the hospital he can expect to see his health further deteriorate.

If my criticism or the metaphor as a whole isn't yet clear, it will become more so as we continue. The underlying factor that I wish to communicate, and prior conservative arguments have failed to address, is that conservatives too have fallen short of our civic obligation to ourselves, and each other. The progressive left has been successful as a result of both a quiet compliance, as well as a failure by conservatives to live up to our social contract, as well. Proponents of states' rights need to concede and recognize the inconsistencies of other so-called likeminded individuals in the historical record, whom of which have furthered their own interests through centralized government. In doing so we not only remain honest in the face of criticism, but also we help ourselves avoid this trap in the future. Precedent for expanding the role of government has no doubt been disproportionately a progressive contribution, but in truth big government has originated from opportunists on both sides, nonetheless. Although I am not in total agreement with the supports of his argument, 19th century historian Henry Adams, emphasized this general political reality even in his era:

"Between the slave power and states' rights there was no necessary connection. The slave power, when in control, was a centralizing influence, and all the most considerable encroachments on states' rights were its acts. The acquisition and admission of Louisiana; the Embargo; the War of 1812; the annexation of Texas "by joint resolution" [rather than treaty]; the war with Mexico, declared by the mere announcement of President Polk; the Fugitive Slave Law; the Dred Scott decision — all triumphs of the slave power — did far more than either tariffs or internal improvements, which in their origin were also southern measures, to destroy the very memory of states' rights as they existed in 1789. Whenever a question arose of extending or protecting slavery, the slaveholders became friends of centralized power, and used that dangerous weapon with a kind of frenzy. Slavery in fact required centralization in order to maintain and protect itself, but it required to control the centralized machine; it needed despotic principles of government, but it needed them exclusively for its own use. Thus, in truth, states' rights were the protection of the free states, and as a matter of fact, during the domination of the slave power, Massachusetts appealed to this protecting principle as often and almost as loudly as South Carolina."[27]

---

[27] Adams, Henry B. *John Randolph.* pg. 270 – 271. 1st Edition. Boston, MA: Houghton Mifflin & Co., 1882

Keeping in line with the metaphor, Doctor Right simply could have done the right thing by voicing to the patient that he has a responsibility for his own health. Ambition, coupled with selfishness and a general lack of virtue prevented both of them from honoring the Hippocratic Oath. This dereliction of duty has not been limited to political leaders, either. Conservative thinkers, as well, have ceded the elementary, secondary, and higher education apparatuses to the progressive left. They have been incompetent and unwillingly to defend the "unchanging and everlasting" principles of the Natural Law. Such selfish consideration, which has been all too present in an academic culture consumed by careerism, has come at the expense of our people's freedom, happiness and well-being. Thus, I will defend the Natural Law at the potential expense to my own career and academic reputation; it wouldn't be the first time my reputation has been in question. However, this discussion will not be constrained by the cage of political correctness, as human nature is not fond of cages of any design. Liberty, of course, is humankind's natural state of happiness, and that applies to both physical and intellectual freedom. The suppression of thought, by any means, is not how free people conduct a national dialogue. As a nation, we are all in this together and, as such, we are all sick. We must all take the medicine that we need to get well… no matter how bitter the taste.

THE PSYCHOLOGY OF VIRTUE

Study colonial America or the national dialogue which transpired before, during, and after our Revolution in a modern academic university, and you will miss a critical element. Only if you were to pour through the primary sources of colonial diaries, personal correspondences and debate records between Continental delegates, would you then understand the true nature of our Founders' struggle. When contemporary Americans speak of terms such as citizenship, the equality of rights, freedom, limited government, and so on, it is with a degree of ignorance, because the whole of society does not understand their origins. Politicians and citizens alike have no understanding of Natural Law, thus both the words and their meaning have become hollow in practice. The implications and consequences from merely professing such ideals have fallen heavily on civil society, as well as resulted in misguided public policy. Whether the matter was concerning day-to-day life, public service to the general welfare, or the prospect of citizenship under new self-governance, at the forefront of their minds was the concept of virtue.

Virtue is said to be of one's character, but is determined by their actions. It is the obligation of one to their Creator, whom of which demands such compulsion, that they will make the happiness of others their duty. Morality, although essential, is insufficient to underscore the behavior that results from virtuous character. Virtuous deeds are inspirational and contagious, as they instill a natural desire among us to imitate those who follow a moral law. We should show affection to family, friends and community, because when we do we please God and serve to promote the general happiness of our society.[28] Lost along with the virtuous obligation to live by a Godly moral law is the understanding that "the most acceptable service we render to Him is in doing good to his other children."[29] Citizens are free to start a family, but parents must care for their children; citizens are free to pursue their own happiness, but neighbors must allow, encourage, and promote the happiness of their fellow-neighbors; individuals are free to prosper, but must acknowledge and carry out their duty to the community as a whole. The concept of virtue has a certain collective element, however, community is not synonymous with collectivism. The Founding Fathers to be sure were 18th century commonwealth men, nevertheless, the modern definition of community would have been insufficient for the protection of individuality. Neither is it the case that the individual is more important than the community *per se*. But individual obligation, or the "calling," must be met on an individual basis.[30] Samuel Adams was never one to split his meaning on the issue of collectivism:

"The Utopian schemes of leveling and a community of goods, are as visionary and impractical as those which vest all property in the Crown. [These ideas] are arbitrary, despotic, and, in our government, unconstitutional."[31]

It is extraordinarily difficult for modern Americans to understand how deeply our Founding Fathers held these beliefs, as anyone who has studied their personal writings can attest. Yet, the actions of Benjamin Franklin help bring us back to a time when such idealism wasn't ignorance, or an unrealistic notion – it was a way of life. Franklin's inventions made him by far the most famous American in the world. Of the Franklin stove, he wrote:

"This Pamphlet had a good Effect, Govr. Thomas was so pleas'd with the Construction of this Stove, as describ'd in it that he offer'd to give me a Patent for the sole Vending of them for a Term of Years; but I declin'd it from a Principle which has ever weigh'd with me on such Occasions, viz., That as we enjoy great Advantages from the Inventions of others, we should be glad of an Opportunity to serve others by any Invention of ours; and this we

---

[28] Weber, Max. *The Protestant Ethic and Spirit of Capitalism.* pg. 115 New York: Rutledge Publishing, 1992
[29] Franklin, Benjamin. *The Writings of Benjamin Franklin.* ed. Smyth, Henry A. Vol. 10 pg. 84 New York: Macmillan Company 1905 – 1907
[30] Ibid. pg. 105 – 106
[31] Adams. Samuel. Quoted from Wells, William V. *The Life and Public Services of Samuel Adams.* Vol. 1 pg. 154 Boston: Little, Brown and Company, 1865

should do freely and generously."[32]

In other words, Franklin understood his needs were well met, as he was wealthy in talent and possession; therefore, he had a duty to see happiness maximized among his fellow-citizens, despite his own personal ambition. The lightening rod and the Franklin Stove, both fulfilled the needs of his countryman and were in extremely high demand, yet he never profited from that demand. He had less worldly motivations for proliferating their use:

"It has pleased God in his goodness to mankind, at length to discover to them the means of securing their habitations and other buildings from mischief by thunder and lightning."[33]

The talents possessed by Benjamin Franklin, he himself, solely credited to God and were to be used for the benefit of all His people. Franklin's generosity was not forced or reinforced by manmade law, nor religious indoctrination *per se*; but it was understood in their Protestant dominated society that obligation to frugality is moral and proper human behavior for free people. The *Protestant Ethic* is the idea that the highest form of moral obligation of the individual is to fulfill his duty in such worldly affairs.[34]

The psychological effects of projecting religious behavior in day-to-day life cannot be understated. Virtues and ethics are all that separated classical American capitalism from the simple pursuit of wealth that transpired in antiquity, European-style capitalism, and the modern American capitalist free market. The secularization of American capitalism has made the pursuit of wealth an end, whereas with Protestantism, wealth historically was a means to achieve a strong civil society. The removal of one's virtuous obligation to "worldly asceticism," or frugality, has made the pursuit of wealth an object of greed.[35] In *Protestant Ethic*, Weber explains:

"On the side of the production of private wealth, asceticism condemned both dishonesty and impulsive avarice. What was condemned as covetousness, Mammonism, etc., was the pursuit of riches for their own sake. For wealth in itself was a temptation."[36]

As with asceticism, the seemingly insignificant removal of the "calling," or the idea we all have a duty to labor to meet our own needs, has had a far-reaching

---

[32] Franklin, Benjamin. *Autobiography of Benjamin Franklin.* pg. 274 Edited by John Bigelow, Philadelphia, PA: J.B. Lippincott & Co., 1869
[33] Franklin, Benjamin. *Poor Richard's Almanack*, 1953. New York: The Heritage Press, 1964
[34] Weber, Max. *The Protestant Ethic and Spirit of Capitalism.* New York: Rutledge Publishing, 1992
[35] Ibid.
[36] Ibid. pg. 116

negative effect on our psychology, thus our collective health.[37] Far too many people simply do not hear that calling, let alone answer. For those who do, too few are fulfilling their obligation to care for the welfare of their fellow-citizens, who have little recourse but to turn to government. A virtuous individual would strive to obtain a position in society where they could serve the needs of the public, as well as ensure that they never become a burden. The right of persons to enjoy a confessed portion of their goods privately in order to grow and contribute to the whole is, of course, a natural right and a natural incentive. Natural Law, which called them to obligation, was "self-evident" and their belief in God's moral law was based upon reason and empirical evidence, rather than some blind acceptance of spiritual revelation. Understanding that there is a worldly and spiritual relationship between our rights and responsibilities is absolutely necessary for a well-run society. In a free and self-governed society, government can only remain limited through limited necessity, thus the business of the public welfare must be a matter of civic obligation. Historian Gordon S. Wood, whose work has helped to preserve a historical record worthy of psychological study, correctly identified that:

"The eighteenth century mind was thoroughly convinced that a popularly based government cannot be supported without virtue."[38]

It appears that contemporary psychology is just now catching up to the 18th century mindset. As it relates to politics, specifically concerning domestic policymaking, the social science field of psychology has long been overlooked and understudied. This is no doubt in large part due to the approach utilized by early studies, which relied upon the discounting of morality, ethics, and the like. Orthodox academics rebuked the idea that these areas are warranted areas of human behavior to study. Freud defined a virtuous person as one who possessed the ability to repress their natural impulses. Nevertheless, virtue was nothing other than a manmade invention, created to separate human beings from other members of the animal kingdom. Freud wrote:

"In the course of his development toward culture, man acquired a dominating position over his fellow creatures in the animal kingdom. Not content with this supremacy, however, he began to place a gulf between his nature and theirs. He denied the possession of reason to them, and to himself he attributed an immortal soul, and made claims to a divine descent which permitted him to annihilate the bond of community between him and the animal

---

[37] Ibid. pg. 106
[38] Wood, Gordon S. *The Creation of the American Republic, 1776 – 1787.* pg. 68 Chapel Hill NC: University of North Carolina Press, 1969

kingdom."[39]

Freudian psychologists emphasize that which is both innate and developed major internal desires, urges, and so on. This component of a man's personality was what Freud referred to as the "id." The "super-ego," or artificially erected cultural artifacts, serves as a countervailing force to the id. The overall personality of an individual was a result of this never-ending battle between the id and the super-ego, which took place within the part of the brain he called man's "ego." The Freudian school of psychoanalysis teaches us much about the inner workings of the human mind, but offers little to explain how we react to the world around us. Also, since morality is manmade, then we have to except that evil or hatred is older than good, love, and the other uniquely agreeable characteristics of human behavior. How does that comport with maternal instinct and affection, or why the suffering of others is so detrimental to our own happiness? Equally insufficient is the Freudian assumption that all id, or animalistic urges are evil. Sexual drive is imperative to ensure the perpetuation of our species. Can sexual drive only be logically categorized as "bad" behavior? Later psychologists, however, ignored these inconveniences and concerned themselves with Freud's inability to identify environmental influences on human behavior.

The Behaviorist approach to the study of human psychology relies upon the objective scientific method. Contrasted with the Freudian method, which focused on internal drives and motivations, Behaviorists are concerned with external environmental stimuli. John B. Watson, the pioneer of the Behaviorist school of psychology, sums up the school of thought:

"Personality is the sum of activities that can be discovered by actual observation of behavior over a long enough time to give reliable information…In other words, personality is but the end product of our habit systems."[40]

It should be expected that Watson and subsequent Behaviorists arrived at this conclusion. When the majority of your experiments were conducted using the white rat as the test subject, the unique elements to human behavior must be ignored by necessity. Instead of building upon the Freudian model, all references to inner desires and motivations were dropped from the vocabulary. While Freud was concerned with subjective analysis, behaviorism pursued only objective studies. That isn't to say there is nothing to be learned from Watson, and later Behaviorists such as Dollard and Miller regarding human influence. Perhaps their greatest contribution, especially concerning the potential effects of public policy,

---

[39] Quoted from *The Third Force: The Psychology of Abraham Maslow.* Goble, Frank G. pg. 14 Chapel Hill NC: Maurice Bassett, 2004
[40] Ibid. pg. 16

may be that we can develop awareness to the good and bad governmental influences in our environment. For instance, such information could be used to fashion policy that inspires productive motivation rather than promote idleness. However, in order to fully understand human potential we need to incorporate, not segregate, all aspects to human behavior. Dismissing that which may not comport with a certain theory is obviously going to result in an incomplete and inapplicable theory. Even if the findings could be used in policymaking, due to missing information, there remains a significant risk that unforeseen consequences may arise.

The ultimate drawback, and our Founding Fathers would have agreed, is that behaviorism is the antithesis to our founding principles. If humans are nothing but a passive product of our environment, then free will and self-determination is a product of our imagination. The supposition that humans are *not* naturally free is essential to their theory.[41] The tendency from both Freudian and Behaviorists – to focus on the link that connects humankind and the animal kingdom – ignores characteristics that are attributable only to human beings. Why do humans strive for betterment and higher being? How is that only humans produce music, artwork, and other forms of artistic creation? It is evident that such capabilities demonstrate that humans have the potential for some higher form of behavior. Contemporary psychologists, particularly Abraham Maslow and Carl Rogers, recognized the incomplete nature of psychological studies and adopted a more comprehensive approach to understand our higher forms of behavior. Maslow had much the same concerns regarding past approaches used by psychoanalysis and behaviorism to study psychology:

"The use of animals guarantees in advance the neglect of just those capacities which are uniquely human for example, martyrdom, self-sacrifice, shame, love, humor, art, beauty, conscience, guilt, patriotism, ideals, the production of poetry or philosophy or music or science. Animal psychology is necessary for learning about those human characteristics that man shares with primates. It is useless in the study of those characteristics which man does not share with other animals, or in which he is vastly superior, such as latent learning."[42]

The reason that psychology is so important for us to understand, is that our entire form of government is based upon our ability to exhibit higher forms of behavior; therefore, legitimately govern ourselves. Freud would not be surprised by the corrupt relationship between politicians and special interest. Instinct to satisfy desires, such as power, wealth and prestige, is natural. Nor would it be particularly shocking for so many Americans to take advantage of the social safety net. Maslow would agree, but pessimism doesn't have to be the end of the story.

[41] Skinner, B. F. *Verbal Behavior.* New York: Appleton-Century-Crofts, 1957
[42] Quoted from *The Third Force: The Psychology of Abraham Maslow.* Goble, Frank G. pg. 27 Chapel Hill NC: Maurice Bassett, 2004

While it is true that humans are capable of debauched motivations, so too is it true that we are designed to experience feelings that almost seem to be an innate cure for our failings. In other words, sometimes we view the world as a glass half full, and sometimes the glass is half empty; but we want to be the people who see it as half full, and if it isn't, then find a way to fill it. The same is true regarding how we view humanity and ourselves. Simply dismissing our optimistic characteristics as mere artificial, self-constructed barriers to the animal kingdom does not sufficiently explain why some feel the need to institute these barriers, while others do not. Maslow said of Freud:

"Freud's picture of man was clearly unsuitable, leaving out as it did his aspirations, his realizable hopes, his godlike qualities...Freud supplied to us the sick half of psychology and we must now fill it out with the healthy half."[43]

For Maslow, as I have charged other areas of academia, conventional wisdom was not wise to the ways of human behavior, at all. Orthodox scientific findings, though useful, are philosophically, historically, and sociologically naïve.[44] Academics have a tendency to excessively specialize in individual areas of study. Instead of collaborating their efforts, they segregate into specialties and compete for the top spot in the academic hierarchy. The primary concern becomes the advancement of their own narrow theories, which of course supports their individual specialty, and at that point loyalties no longer lay with the discovery of whole truth.

In any area of study, the approach that incorporates the credible elements of past individual studies without discrimination, is the one in which truth is paramount. Prior to the 19th century, psychology was the realm of philosophers and theologians. Science, religion, morality, and so on, were not polar opposites. They operated within the same sphere, each serving a role in the pursuit of a greater understanding of ourselves and the world around us. In this spirit of cohesion, Maslow and other psychologists who have followed his approach, sought a more comprehensive means to study psychology that is applicable to political and historical behaviors. This approach, called humanism, is a more tenable method to study higher forms of human behavior, such as those exhibited by our Founding Fathers. Its emphasis on free will and self-determination is a more conducive application to the American ideal, as well as a means to provide insight to how America became the historical anomaly it is.

If virtue is a cultural barrier, as Freud professed, then we should expect the Founders to have submitted to their id and dismantle those barriers. They certainly were in the position to reinvent our cultural norms. Instead, they chose

---

[43] Ibid. pg. 28
[44] Maslow, Abraham H. *The Psychology of Science; a Reconnaissance.* Chapel Hill NC: Maurice Bassett, 2002

to implement legal restrictions for their own potential power, for those who were to follow them, and laid the groundwork for future generations to be educated in the principles and tenets of Natural Law.[45] Are we to suppose Freud merely overlooked this inconsistency when he studied historical figures? Likewise, the need to adopt the Bill of Rights would have been unnecessary if human beings were a passive product of their environment. The reality of human nature, as our Founders understood it, is that human behavior is too complex to exclusively limit to either internal or external influences. Freud is correct to observe the existence of deeply embedded desires, of which many are wicked in their nature and strongly motivate human behavior. Humans, as well, are reactionary to the environment around them as Watson observed. However, we are also constantly and aggressively influencing our surrounding environment. Yet, it is inadequate to find explanation for all human behavior in a hybrid version of the two schools, as well. Neither school of psychology alone, nor an interwoven hybrid of the two, can account for the self-denial of power displayed by Washington in his decision to leave the Office of the President. What remains unique to humans, which is of the utmost importance, is the conscience ability to reason which influence is acting upon us at any given time and resist impulsive behavior. If the internal influence of Freud is the first, and the external force of Behaviorists is the second, then the natural influence of reason is indeed a component of the "third force" on human behavior.

An individual's heightened degree of awareness to said influences will increase their power of self-determination. Humanistic psychologists refer to those who possess this mental maturity as "self-actualized" individuals. Maslow describes this journey of "self-actualization" to which individuals embark on:

"What a man can be, he must be. This need we may call self-actualization...It refers to the desire for self-fulfillment, namely, to the tendency for him to become actualized in what he is potentially. This tendency might be phrased as the desire to become more and more what one is, to become everything that one is capable of becoming."[46]

Founders such as Benjamin Franklin and Thomas Jefferson were poster children for the study of self-actualized individuals. This type of person has a habit of approaching problems with a diverse amount of seemingly unrelated information. In professional endeavors, they use their desire to collaborate and unify in order to create, invent, and discover new previously unrealized human possibilities. As was the case with our original Founding Father George Washington, a high capacity for self-reliance makes them individualistic and ambitious. Yet, they

---

[45] *Federal and State Constitutions: Colonial Charters, and Other Organic Laws of the States, Territories, and Colonies, Now or Heretofore Forming the United States of America.* Vol. 2 Washington DC: US Government Printing Office, 1909

[46] Maslow, Abraham. *A Theory of Human Motivation.* pg. 370 – 396 Psychological Review #50 1943

exhibit the most obligation to society as a whole, and display greater than normal affection to their fellow-neighbors. They strive for harmony and community, but are not hesitant to take principled positions and resist societal changes when they stand in contrast to what they know to be an absolute truth. They hold deeply rooted beliefs in a meaningful universe, where moral law exists as a matter of Natural Law, or what they at least know simply to be human nature. These beliefs, which the self-actualized base on reason and personal experience, coincide with the tenets of religious teachings. It has been observed that these beliefs produce a self-fulfilling and wellness-producing state of mind, which leads to a higher form of human behavior:

"e.g., the transcendence of self, the fusion of the true, the good and the beautiful, contribution to others, wisdom, honesty, and naturalness, the transcendence of selfish and personal motivations, the giving up of 'lower' desires in favor of 'higher' ones,...the decrease of hostility, cruelty, and destructiveness and the increase of friendliness, kindness, etc."[47]

Humanistic psychology has rediscovered what would have been recognized in the 18th century as the pursuit of virtue and enlightenment. Although they were clearly unaware of the term "hierarchy of needs," as Maslow later deemed the process, they pursued the same course with the same intention.[48] The fulfillment of our most basic human needs of a physiological nature, such as breathing, water, food, etc., is one's own natural obligation for ensuring the survival of self, family and species. When we are hungry for food, we are hungry not only in our stomach, but we are hungry "all over" and consumed with the desire to fulfill that need.[49] The same is true for sex, sleep, and so on. As we climb the hierarchy of needs the same phenomena persists. When we seek out our basic needs for shelter, protection and safety, we are again consumed, because of the need to achieve a means of security; lest we find ourselves in a vulnerable state of being or no state at all. Nature provides us with validation when we fulfill these needs through certain observations within ourselves. If we fail to meet a basic need, then the presence of physical illness arises i.e., physiological deficiencies, or malnourishment. Physiological illnesses, however, are also accompanied by psychological deficiencies and unhealthy mental behavior. The absence of fulfillment results in inactive behavior, "at a low ebb," and the inability to

---

[47] Quoted from *The Third Force: The Psychology of Abraham Maslow.* Goble, Frank G. pg. 43 Chapel Hill NC: Maurice Bassett, 2004

[48] Reference to the stages of human mental growth, beginning with basic physiological needs, and ending at self-actualization, or an enlightened fulfillment of one's potential.

[49] Quoted from *The Third Force: The Psychology of Abraham Maslow.* Goble, Frank G. pg. 50 Chapel Hill NC: Maurice Bassett, 2004

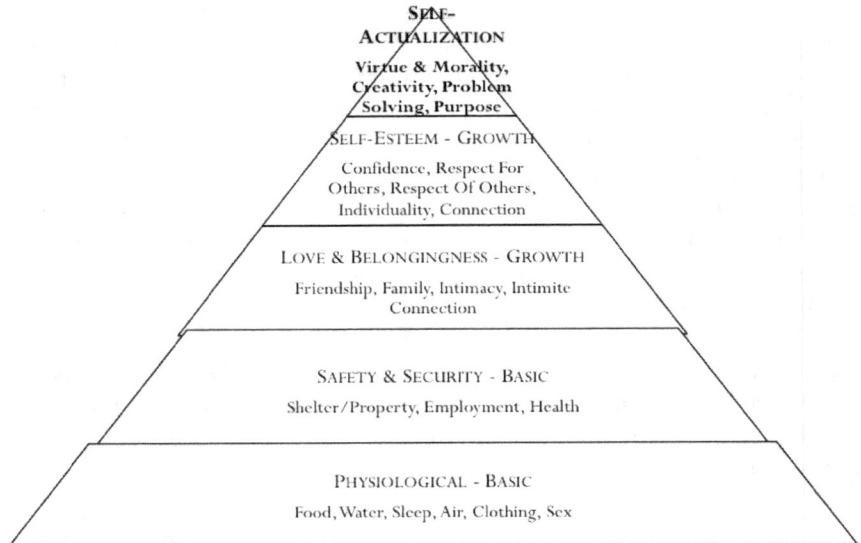

Figure 1.1: Maslow's "Hierarchy Of Needs," in which only our basic needs – physiological, safety and security – can even hope to be met by government, leaving behind personal growth and the benefits of natural validation that results from meeting our growth needs.

perform other competent functionalities that are present in a healthy person.[50] As we ascend up the hierarchy, a third force continues to act upon us to meet our ever-worthy demands. The need to love and be loved, self-esteem, and ultimately the pursuit of a state of contentment or completion and the understanding of truth, all strengthen our self-sufficient individual being; in which, we physically and mentally enjoy a healthy and happy existence.

Pursuits of self-sufficiency, self-fulfillment, and general betterment are necessary on an individual basis if a collective unit hopes to prosper. Without virtue, which the self-actualized were all found to possess, society will simply become too unhealthy for self-governance. As we ascend to meet our "growth needs," such as individuality, self-sufficiency and the pursuit of truth, the hunger "all over" relies upon certain deeply held convictions. Proponents of the "New Atheists" dismiss the religious belief in God as a delusional artifact, or a mere superstition of antiquity. But the real path to the pursuit of truth should be expected to follow the same pattern as all other human needs. That is to say, natural beliefs and behaviors in the pursuit of truth and other growth needs should result in the same natural validations, or benefits to human health and behavior. Conversely, we should expect nothing less than the opposite to occur, or a negative impact on health and well-being when we choose to push against Natural Law and truth. The correlation between health and religion has firmly

---

[50] Ibid. pg. 54

been established in studies of public opinion.[51] Frank Newport has suggested that an increase in religiosity among Americans is likely as more Americans begin to become aware of the benefits to our physical and psychological well-being.[52] The evidence, however, is not relegated to the social science arena as I have myself relied upon up thus far. Medical studies have provided a plethora of evidence for the relationship between religious participation and health, albeit its infancy has caused a resistance to an out-right proclamation as to *why* the phenomenon exists. Nevertheless, their work has provided significant evidence of this relationship, and frankly I would be skeptical of science's ability or credibility to provide a *whole* answer for either the *how* or *why* this phenomenon transpires.

Throughout the last century, over 200 epidemiologic and clinical studies have documented the influence of religious affiliation on physical and mental well-being. For a degree of reasons, some of which are ill-intended, the publications that find the relationship to exist have not been widely distributed, nor are they reflected in modern public policy. To some extent, the purposes of the studies were simply not specified for this cause, but the data are available regardless:

"Across this literature, however, the consistency of findings despite the diversity of samples, designs, methodologies, religious measures, health outcomes, and population characteristics actually serve to strengthen the inference of a positive association between religion and health. This finding has been observed in studies of old, middle-aged, and young respondents; in men and women; in subjects from the United States, Europe, Africa, and Asia; in research conducted in the 1930s and into the 1990s; in case-control, prospective cohort, cross-sectional, and panel studies; in Protestants, Catholics, Jews, Muslims, Buddhists, Parsis, and Zulus; in studies operationalizing religiosity as any of over a dozen variables (religious attendance, prayer, Bible reading, church membership, subjective religiousness, Yeshiva education, etc.); in research limited to t tests and bivariate correlations and in research testing structural-equation models with LISREL; and in U.S. studies, among Anglo-whites, Hispanics, Asian Americans, and African Americans (Levin, 1994a). The volume of more systematic study of the 'epidemiology of religion' (Levin & Vanderpool, 1987)."[53]

The natural verification process that we unconsciously rely upon for validation when we have fulfilled our basic human needs is also applicable to our growth needs. Unlike our basic needs, however, the validation is not as obvious, thus we must simply make a conscious effort to observe it. Religion, as a means to fulfill our growth needs, is clearly validated through Natural Law in the same manner

---

[51] Newport, Frank. *God is Alive and Well: The Future of Religion in America.* Gallup Press, 2012

[52] Ibid.

[53] Levin, Jeffrey S. and Chatters, Linda M. *Research on Religion and Mental Health: An Overview of Empirical Findings and Theoretical Issues.* pg. 34 – 35. *Handbook of Religion and Mental Health.* Edited by Harold G. Koenig. Elsevier, 1998

as our basic needs. Meeting or failing to meet our growth needs results in the same benefits or consequences that are observable through our basic needs. The same manner we prevent falling ill when we satisfy our thirst and hunger, so too do we exhibit health in our mental and physical well-being from religious observation. The wealth of data displaying broad application among humans as a whole species is significant. Aside from its consistency with our American ideals, it suggests that regardless of our differences in region, race, or era there is a universal Natural Law that applies to us all; from which, we can observe whether or not our conduct is a truly healthy means to fulfill our growth needs. How we choose to fulfill the need to love and be loved, or to belong, can mean all of the difference between being in a healthy, or unhealthy relationship; the difference between drug addiction, or sobriety; the consumption of food for sustenance, or in excess to obesity; the difference between frugality, or debt-prone spending habits, and so on.

My argument for the presence of "natural validations" is also corroborated by the research of Michael Blume, who demonstrated that people of faith out-produce their secular counterparts, causing adamant proponents of "dual-inheritance theory" – such as Sue Blackmore – to out-right proclaim they were wrong.[54] Atheist "scholar" Richard Dawkins, who suggested that religions are "viruses of the mind" that infect and impose great costs in terms of money, time and health, is wrong. "It is a great irony but evolution appears to discriminate against Atheists and favor those with religious beliefs," and since "most societies or communities that have espoused atheistic beliefs have not survived more than a century," their chosen approach to the pursuit of truth, ultimately condemns their cause.[55] Just as we can expect to become ill from denying our basic physiological needs, Atheist or others who refuse to observe Nature Law can expect to be excluded from realizing this natural benefit to their health and well-being – an indeed, they are.[56]

An empirical revelation of such significance, in which we are all cut from the same spiritual cloth so to speak, is obviously present for further observation. However, in the same fashion that Maslow found flaw with excessive specialization, so too do Levin and Chatters. Rather than honoring the Hippocratic Oath by following the data wherever it may take their research, medical studies have consciously avoided the study of religion for political and material considerations. Medical fields of research, undoubtedly, practice a policy of hostility toward the careers of those who may have concluded that the

---

[54] Blackmore, Sue. *Why I no longer believe religion is a virus of the mind*. On "Explaining Religion" Conference in *The Guardian*. September 16th, 2010.

[55] Blume, Michael: "The Reproductive Advantage of Religiosity - Bristol 2010", Lecture at the "Explaining Religion" Conference, Bristol University 2010

[56] Lim, Chaeyoon. *Gallup-Healthways Well-Being Index: In U.S. Churchgoers Boast Better Mood, Especially on Sundays*. March 22nd, 2012

study of truth is a worthwhile endeavor; that is of course, if that pursuit should lead them to "the R word," or religion as a potential preventative treatment for mental or physical disorders:

"Psychiatric researchers in considerable numbers apparently agree that religious involvement is worth studying as a potential protective or risk factor, yet they are reluctant to pursue these questions or are unsure of how to proceed in the absence of widespread dissemination of prior findings and theoretical work. Another significant factor may be the perception that consideration of "the R word" (Larson, Sherrill, & Lyons, 1994) represents an "anti-tenure factor" (Sherrill & Larson, 1994) for academic psychiatrists. According to Peck (1993), in an address to the American Psychiatric Association in 1992, "Psychiatry has not only neglected but actively ignored the issue of spirituality" (p. 233), a situation he termed "psychiatry's predicament" (p. 232)."[57]

The name M. Scott Peck, author of *The Road Less Traveled* and referenced by Levin and Chatters, may be synonymous with a string of "self-help" books in popular culture, but Peck was a renowned psychiatrist whose work professed the benefits to an American revival espousing many tenets found in the Protestant ethic. Peck observed that it is the nature of the human condition for us to avoid our problems, however, ignoring or deferring only serves to exacerbate them. Self-discipline, delayed gratification, the acceptance of duty and responsibility for our actions, can all be combined with a lifestyle of Spirit and active love, which is our natural means to transform our weakness into strength.[58] Although due credit must be given to certain political figures of the era and their policies, Peck's work was instrumental in the revival of the Protestant ethic during the 1980s and 1990s. Peck also co-founded the nonprofit organization, the Foundation for Community Encouragement, which has a stated mission "to teach the principle of community to individuals and organizations."[59] During the 7 years from 2002 – 2009, the organization had ceased their day-to-day operations, but now they have reopened their doors to offer community-building and individual training events to churches, schools, government agencies, prisons, universities and businessmen.

Peck, in essence, put into practice that which the Founders foresaw as the need for civil institutions to teach the virtuous obligation to community. Society, as a whole, clearly has only two choices when determining how the needs of the community will be met; through civil action within the community, or to delegate their responsibility to government. Studies have thoroughly established that the happiness of the whole community impacts whether or not an individual

---

[57] Ibid. pg. 35

[58] Peck, M. Scott. *The Road Less Traveled: A New Psychology of Love, Traditional Values and Spiritual Growth.* Simon & Shuster, 1978

[59] Jones, Arthur. *The Road He Travelled: The Revealing Biography of M. Scott Peck.* Rider, 2007

reports their own happiness, health and well-being.[60] Indeed, both happiness and misery are contagious, thus the popular expression which observes, "misery likes company." It is undeniably true that the closer the relationship the greater the suffering of other human beings will impact our own well-being. But as it has been correctly argued, it is also true that it is in our nature to avoid or defer our problems. As it relates to poverty, for instance, domestic social welfare policy is a manifestation of that deference. Rather than taking "the road less traveled," taxpayers have reconciled the inaction, or insufficiency of present civil action through their tax burden.[61] That is to say, although suffering in society is difficult to witness, it can often be just as difficult if not more, to resolve. Therefore, it should come as little surprise that politicians who promise collective action to fulfill any of our hierarchy of needs are naturally successful. Unfortunately, the government method itself is neither natural, nor successful.

Unlike government, caring for the well-being of the community through civil institutions satisfies the necessary human elements to happiness without sacrificing individual sovereignty, identity, or personal liberty. Government, by necessity, must regulate and tax in order to meet the obligation forfeited by *We the People*, which is further deteriorating our natural state of happiness and well-being – liberty. Furthermore, no natural validation is attained from deferring our civic duty to government. We do not benefit either physically or emotionally, because shrinking from our obligation does not require personal growth, thus does not meet any of our higher growth needs. Neither instant nor delayed gratification is achieved when we defer to government our own obligation to maintain a just society; one in which, individuals can pursue the healthy connections we desire, while simultaneously experiencing an individual sense of accomplishment. Growth needs such as the need for justice, to love and be loved, are needs that must be witnessed and carried out by direct intimacy if we are to grow in ourselves. A just society is successful at providing for the needs of other citizens, but in an unjust society, we never care to witness the just improvement to another's well-being. Thus, even if government action was successful, by its nature it lacks the intimacy we need to experience real gratification, or fulfill the to desire to instill happiness in others. This system, as we can observe today, is one in which selfishness runs rampant as individuals increasingly withdraw into themselves. On the other hand, being specifically associated with the Protestant ethic is the call to duty and responsibility, obligation to community, and the summoning to personal growth through virtue, morality and the observation of God's Natural Law. This journey is a spiritual

---

[60] Agrawal, Sangeeta and Harter, James K. *Wellbeing Meta-Analysis: A Worldwide Study of the Relationship Between the Five Elements of Wellbeing and Life Evaluation, Daily Experiences, Health, and Giving.* Gallup: World Poll Analysis. April, 2011.

[61] Peck, M. Scott. *The Road Less Traveled: A New Psychology of Love, Traditional Values and Spiritual Growth.* pg. 1 Simon & Shuster, 1978

one, requires personal growth, and results in our happiness and well-being. It is also an individual event, which too can present the danger of an overly selfish society if we place too great an emphasis on the journey solely for one's own purpose. The Founding Fathers would have responded with the proposition to think of the individual's journey for the sake of the whole, but take care not to lose ourselves in the collective trap, which ensures a petty and selfish society. This is a delicate balance to be sure, but with a proper understanding of our own human nature, the nature of government and Natural Law, a society of Spirit can constantly strive for equilibrium.

What does it take to ensure that the community as a whole will meet their obligation? The observation of religion, we have established, results in the development of healthy mental attributes and the belief in a natural moral law, which is of paramount importance to how we choose to fulfill our needs. Life, liberty, and the pursuit of happiness could easily become the pursuit of selfishness, and I contend it has. Gandhi wrestled with how to explain the spiritual need for morality as it pertains to society and governance, and ultimately, he came to the same conclusion; "to observe morality is to attain mastery over our mind and our passion," which serves to ensure a person will "conduct himself in such a way that his behavior will not hamper the well-being of his neighbors."[62] Gandhi shared the realization with our Founders that any government promise to fulfill societies' needs was a farce, and must be acknowledged as such so it may be supplemented with another mean, as the only true promise of government is despotism. He was educated in England and agreed with the Western philosophical premise that "God gifted man with intellect so that he might know his Maker," but the West was trending away from the principles of the Enlightenment toward secularization, and that led him to believe that the modern political nature "of the Western civilization is to propagate immorality."[63] Nature, history, and reason all tell us there is no real expectation for us to follow a moral law when we do not observe the source of that law. From within this moral law we derive our obligation to others. Virtue is but a byproduct of the obedience to this law. Virtue, indeed, is the natural remedy for our happiness in a community body.

These ideals were so strongly held that the proper function of society, thus our government, was contingent upon principled living. As redistributionist governments repeatedly prove, private property is a necessary incentive to work since the law cannot force society to be productive. Empowerment and the right to private occupation does encourage the fulfillment of each individual's work duty obligation – or calling. The spoils of their talents, education, and hard work came in the form of economic independence. Upon examination, "the lessons of

---

[62] Gandhi, Mohandas, Karamchand. *Enlightened Anarchy*. Selection from "Nations and Identities." Edited by Vincent Pecora. pg. 207, 215 Malden, MA: Blackwell Publishers, 2001
[63] Ibid. pg. 209, 213

history indicated that without an economically independent, educated, leisured order of society standing securely and permanently above the petty selfishness and multitudes" that exist in pure democracy and collectivism, society self-destructs.[64] Members of society at such a station, coupled with "psychological freedom," can better provide public service absent monetary ambition.[65] Private success was not envied or criticized, it was celebrated, just so long as the individual remained committed to the principle of community and satisfied their civic obligations.

Thomas Jefferson wrote extensively regarding what he called a "natural aristocracy" juxtaposed to the "artificial aristocracy" found throughout the governments of Europe. These were individual citizens who possessed enormous talent and virtue, which regardless of ancestral class should be nurtured through education to later serve the greater public interest. Jefferson's natural aristocracy is synonymous with the individuals in the Humanist studies of the self-actualized. Virtuous leaders being necessary for public virtue, a consensus developed among our Founders that the best form of government is designed to recognize these individuals in society. Jefferson wrote:

"For promoting the public happiness, those persons who nature has endowed with genius and virtue, should be rendered by liberal education worthy to receive, and able to guard the sacred deposit of the rights and liberties of their fellow citizens; and they should be called to that charge without regard to... birth, or other accidental condition or circumstance."[66]

This has clearly not been a priority of public education in modern America. Ignorance to these ideals has allowed an artificial aristocracy to establish itself in both state and federal bodies of government. Career politicians are more common inhabitants of our governments than those belonging to Jefferson's "natural aristocracy." This is due in part to the rent-seeking behavior that accelerated after the passage of the 17th Amendment, which will be discussed further in chapter 2, but abandoning the practice of principled education in Natural Law has had severe ramifications on the balance between unalienable rights and unalienable duties in our waning civil society. The corrupting nature of high office incentivizes the powerful to prevent others in society from ever obtaining similar power. Leadership behavior, as our Founders stressed, has a profound effect on tone, political discourse, and behavior among and between individual citizens in society. As Washington wrote, "Example, whether it be

---

[64] Bailyn, Bernard. *The Ideological Origins of the American Revolution.* pg. 284 Cambridge, MA: Belknap of Harvard University Press, 1992

[65] Reference to virtuous or "self-actualized" individuals, who possess the ability to make their own moral decisions in spite of contrary popular opinion or cultural norms.

[66] Jefferson, Thomas. *The Writing of Thomas Jefferson.* Edited by Paul Leicester Ford. Vol. 2 pg. 221 New York: G.P. Putnam's Sons. 1892 – 1899

good or bad, has a powerful influence".[67]

Resulting from this inequality of opportunity is social immobilization, resentment, and the creation of a platform from which redistributionist politicians can preach progressivism. Put simply, people begin to wonder why they operate honestly when their leaders and fellow-citizens do not. The natural inclination is to begin to question how much effort should be dedicated to labor when the spoils are hoarded, and civic work duty goes unrewarded – or even punished. Although redistribution will only serve to exacerbate inequality, as the historical record shows, the rhetoric has a natural appeal to our individual desire to meet our basic needs. Ultimately, this is the area in which I take issue with part of Maslow's conclusions. Classifying our human needs into the separate categories of basic and growth needs is what enables us to study those "which are uniquely human." His observation of a natural physiological and psychological validation from the fulfillment of basic needs, which I have demonstrated applies to growth needs as well when we observe religion, and indeed his logical premise for the need to study the healthy, are all valid. I do not, however, observe the strict hierarchy as Maslow did. Economic well-being, from which we can better secure our basic needs, is not necessarily a prerequisite to happiness or self-actualization.[68] Furthermore, as professed in the Protestant ethic, wealth can produce idleness and misery just as easily as it can provide a state of well-being. Therefore, adapting alternatives to the pursuit of wealth for wealth's sake is the objective; after all, "money can't buy you love" or happiness, thus the wretched state of Hollywood, CA, and the District of Columbia. Money, itself, is often misused to fulfill our need to belong, to be loved, or even to fulfill our basic needs in an unhealthy and unproductive manner. Instead, the pursuit of the Spirit is paramount, while wealth is for the betterment of the whole of society.

The fact that the survival of liberty would be contingent upon future generations understanding the importance of virtue did not escape them. Samuel Adams, often referred to as the father of the American Revolution, wrote concerning future generations to Richard Henry Lee, "I thank God that I have lived to see my country independent and free. She may long enjoy her freedom and independence if she will. It depends on her virtue."[69]

Even if scientific critics could prove virtue is just a cultural artifact, which they cannot, that still would not amount to its nonexistence. For instance, nationalism has long been argued to be a cultural artifact, nevertheless, truly does exist.[70] Liberal historiographer, Hugh Seton-Watson, despite his best efforts

---

[67] Washington, George. *Letter to Lord Stirling* March 5th, 1780. See Writings…

[68] Diener, Ed. International Difference in Well-Being. pg. 217 – 245 Oxford University Press, 2010

[69] Wells, William V. *The Life and Public Services of Samuel Adams*. Vol. 3 pg. 175 Boston: Little, Brown and Company, 1865

[70] Anderson, Benedict. *Imagined Communities*. New Edition. New York: Verso, 2006

reluctantly admitted that he was "driven to the conclusion that no 'scientific definition' of the nation can be devised; yet the phenomenon has existed and exists."[71]

Perhaps, had these academics not been too preoccupied with their own narrow disciplines, then they would have been more versed in other intellectual approaches and observations. Either way, our Founders most assuredly did believe in the truth of virtue, and its importance in reaching a proper balance between the individual and community; and thus, designed our system of government to hinge upon the philosophy of the Protestant ethic and Natural Law. It is unrealistic to expect every citizen to pursue and reach self-actualized status, but within government at least, the natural aristocracy should far outweigh those who pursue petty ambitions. Every citizen, however, was and still is realistically expected to understand and practice basic civic virtue, answer their duty of calling, and practice a certain level of frugality as demanded by worldly asceticism. The American social contract was established with as many duties as rights, which due to conditions to be discussed further in chapter 3, society as a whole has forgotten. Virtue, it was expected, each person should struggle toward as a part of citizenship. In order to prevent "fundamentally transforming" the social contract, which from Rousseau we can discern will result in consequence, it is necessary for a strong civil society to retain our national ethic. Yet, an expectation for the same limitation on government persists in the minds of so many Americans, particularly conservatives, while at the same time the danger of further expanding the role of government is absent in the minds of other Americans. In the following section we will identify key implications on American citizenship from the aforementioned ideals, the dangers posed to individual sovereignty from government as dictated by the Natural Law, and how our failure to acknowledge "it summons to duty by its commands" has threatened the state of our union.[72]

INDIVIDUAL CITIZENSHIP, OBLIGATION TO COMMUNITY, & THE STATE OF OUR UNION

Proponents of progressivism will no doubt charge my argument with providing evidence based on archaic notions such as Natural Law, and failing to adequately highlight the shortfalls of our nation's founding. They will point to exclusions placed on citizenship, and predictably, the restriction of rights for minorities and women in early American history. Uprooting the only political

[71] Seton-Watson, Hugh. *Nations and States. An Enquiry into the Origins of Nations and the Politics of Nationalism.* pg. 5 Boulder, CO: Westview Press, 1977
[72] Ebenstein, William. *Great Political Thinkers.* pg. 131 New York: Holt, Rinehart and Winston, 1963

system known to them for what was considered a radical experiment in self-governance, explains many of the charges their critics put forward. Responding to Abigail's letter in 1776, John Adams wrote regarding the request to codify the equal rights of women:

"As to your extraordinary Code of Laws, I cannot but laugh. We have been told that our Struggle has loosened the bands of Government every where. That Children and Apprentices were disobedient – that schools and Colledges were grown turbulent – that Indians slighted their Guardians and Negroes grew insolent to their Masters... I begin to think the Ministry as deep as they are wicked. After stirring up Tories, Landjobbers, Trimmers, Bigots, Canadians, Indians, Negroes, Hanovverians, Hessians, Russians, Irish Roman Catholic, Scotch Renegades, at last they have stimulated the [text missing] to demand new Priviledges and threaten to rebel."[73]

When we criticize our founding documents and those who created them for exclusions of personhood, it is important to understand that the world in which our Founders were living had literally been turned upside down. The fear of mob rule was present, and justified. Who in the end would it have served for them to have made decisions, whether real or imagined, that threatened to tear the fragile fabric of society apart, potentially undoing their efforts?

The academic literature claims that one of the stated goals of the progressive agenda is the forming, and subsequent ensuring, of a more inclusive society. Through government action, citizenship and rights can be protected for those who have been unable to fully participate, or be recognized in society. In reality, government action has never been the instrument to initiate meaningful promotions of social equality. Civil rights legislation has been the result of our communities – pure in their intentions – acting on a commitment to our society living up to American ideals. Legislation driven by public opinion to preserves personhood forces the government to recommit to our founding principles. If the relationship between the citizen and the State remains in the traditional sense without bypassing the traditional institutions of civil society, which is the pattern with grassroots movements, it does not change the terms of our social contract. Government initiated reforms are largely economic-based programs designed to increase dependency, and redefine the relationship between the individual citizen and the State.

To clarify, a citizen is typically understood as a legally recognized free person who possesses individual sovereignty, that is the right to one's life, body, and labor. If these parameters to define citizenship were sufficient, then it is logical to conclude that government may be utilized as a benign or benevolent force for equality. But this is a very narrow understanding of the term citizenship. By this

---

[73] *Letter to Abigail Adams.* April 14th 1776. *Adams Family Correspondence.* Edited by L.H. Butterfield. Vol. 1 pg. 381 Cambridge, MA: Harvard University Press 1963

definition, there is little to differentiate a citizen from an *old world* subject.[74] There are three elements to citizenship, of which the first two have consumed our attention. The third element, however, has been completely absent from any discussion.

Individual sovereignty, or what our Founders referred to as one's natural right, is the first element of citizenship commonly referred to as "personhood." The right to life, or to exist; the right to liberty, or to exist in a state absent oppression; and of course, the pursuit of happiness, which is the right to possess property or the fruits of our own labor; all of which, are God-given and revocable only by Him. However, governments attempt and succeed in their attempts to revoke these rights through hard or soft coercion. The second element of citizenship is the assurance of our personhood against said attempts through "rights of protection" such as suffrage, the right to sue, bear arms, to be eligible for office, due process, and so on. The ability to protect our natural rights is not only necessary for them to have meaning and staying power, but is an acknowledgement by government that it is understood from where we derive them. In the American social contract, government cedes this self-evident truth, thus we possess the power to take recourse in the event that Natural Law is violated. Even though our government acknowledges natural rights are God-given by codifying them as such in our founding documents, if we believe the State to be the source of our rights, then we have no standing to contest the State when it inevitably deems it necessary to restrict or revoke them. Therefore, we should expect any attempt from despotic government to subvert our rights would include a concerted push for secularization.

This is where the general consensus ends and the argument begins between the conservative and progressive ideologies. Deriving the right to personhood from government and not God, no matter the intent, is a counter-logical argument. Laying claim to a "moral imperative," will not exempt society from inevitable government overreach.[75] Progressive legal historian Barbara Young Welke, claims this practice of deference to the supremacy of government law:

"...holds out the promise of a progressive, liberal narrative: as the borders of belonging expand, those outside are brought in... It is to say that with the creation and expansion of the modern liberal state, law has operated as an authoritative discourse, that it fundamentally shapes individual identity and rights, relationship among individuals, and

---

[74] Reference to European relationship to the state who provides persons with rights. Compared to the American social contract that acknowledges these rights are derived by God. Thus, the state has no authority to take them away. i.e. Hobbes v. Locke

[75] Reference to the term or phrase used by progressives to justify government necessity at the expense of individual liberties.

the relationship among individuals to the state."[76]

Although Welke's work does identify the relationship between the first and second elements of citizenship, she refuses to explore the consequences of such an authoritative role for government. In fact, one cannot help but detect a naïve celebratory tone in her work. Should the State serve to define the relationship between individuals? If the State shapes the boundaries of direct relationships between the government and individuals, then will something critical be left out? What consequence could this have on society collectively? While all of these questions will be further explored and the consequences identified with detail in chapters to follow, for the benefit of discussing citizenship, the deriving of rights from the State is most relevant.

Welke and other progressive revisionists have argued that early American law created boundaries intended to exclude people based on race, gender, and disability. However, the "modern liberal state" – by that she means the federal government – has not been particularly effective at expanding the "borders of belonging" through legal coercion. In fact, the power of the State has been used disproportionately to restrict rights, especially in the modern era. By her admission, the 19th century was a period marked by persistent legal action directed at expanding the equality of rights to black Americans and women. In 1868, Congress adopted the 14th Amendment granting due process and equal protection, or natural rights, yet black Americans were still denied suffrage. A mere two years later in 1870, the 15th Amendment guaranteed the rights of all citizens to vote, or a right of protection, but it did not extend to women nor prevent voter discrimination. *Plessy v. Ferguson* (1896), rendered the 14th Amendment irrelevant by establishing *separate but equal*.[77] Similarly, the prior ruling in *Minor v. Happersett* (1875) blatantly rejected a women's right to vote despite the language of both the 14th and 15th Amendments.[78]

The ineffectiveness of top-down, or government-centered solutions is both natural and to be expected when we understand from where our rights are derived. Centralization cannot expand the borders of belonging, because meaningful societal reforms must come from the natural bottom-up process, which begins with *We the People* and our individual communities. Imposing top-down policies only serves to create greater social disorder, much the same way *Roe v. Wade* (1973) has failed to resolve the issue of abortion. As we will address in the following chapter, federal intervention during Reconstruction further exacerbated social disorder in the South. Nevertheless, even though abolition and women's suffrage are seen as adjoining struggles, competing for centralized

---

[76] Welke, Barbara Young. *Law and the Borders of Belonging in the Long Nineteenth Century United States.* pg. 6 Cambridge University Press, 2010

[77] *Plessy v. Ferguson* 163 U.S. 537 (1896)

[78] *Minor v. Happersett* 88 U.S. 162 (1875)

solutions made obtaining natural rights a zero-sum game. The advancement of abolitionism came at the expense to women's rights.

The State does not have the natural authority to issue natural rights to citizens they deem deserving, but it does have the natural inclination to restrict them. The 19th Amendment, which ultimately recognized a woman's right to vote, was an affirmation of a bottom-up movement that originated in our natural political territory – communities. Citizens educated on the origin of natural rights demanded society follow the Laws of Nature and Nature's God. Beginning within communities in Kentucky in 1838, women were granted the authority to vote in school board elections. The movement spread to ten other states as a response to both federal and state judicial failures, with Wyoming affording women's suffrage on an equal basis with men.[79] Unlike the unnatural top-down approach taken with black American voting rights, social backlash to women's suffrage did not reach the level of societal dysfunction that was witnessed in the South.

From thinking about citizenship in these terms, comes the understanding that if we rely on the government to grant us permission to possess our natural rights, or the rights of basic personhood, then we are also subject to their revocation at anytime. Under this new social contract, citizens merely hope that the State decides to tolerate the rights of protection that are necessary to ensure the existence of our natural rights. There is no further need of the law to provide for the equal protection of our natural rights, because further legislation could only create new borders to exclude other citizens. What if the State decided that some people have too much or too little individual sovereignty? The needs of the State are not static, but dynamic. What if it benefits the needs of the State, at any particular time, to restrict the personhood of some but not of others? Ultimately, this is what the progressive argument assails, that this in fact was, and still is the legal reality in America. Yet, their solution is to grant government even more authority and trust that the moral imperative will serve as a check and balance. If the progressive argument states that law was used to establish legal relationships, which preserved inequality, then now that the legal language is corrected society can be free to move toward the proliferation of knowledge as this issue relates to the Natural Law:

"Those rights, then, which God and nature have established, and are therefore called natural rights, such as are life and liberty, need not the aid of human laws to be more effectually invested in every man than they are; neither do they receive any additional strength when declared by the municipal laws to be inviolable."[80]

---

[79] Flexner, Eleanor. *Century of Struggle: The Woman's Rights Movement in the United States*. Cambridge, MA: Belknap of Harvard University Press, 1975

[80] Blackstone, William. Commentaries on the Laws of England. Edited by William Carey Jones. Vol. 1 pg. 93 San Francisco: Bancroft – Whitney Co., 1916

It is logical to conclude that the intention is not simply to abolish these early legal relationships, but also to abuse the law to reverse the roles for social retribution. Redefining the relationship between the individual and the State has done much to undermine the final and imperative element to American citizenship.

The third element of citizenship is rooted in a belief in the existence of Natural Law, hinges upon the fulfillment of the obligations that are outlined in the ethic, and collapses our entire system of liberty-protecting republican government when ignored. Citizens are obligated to balance out their rights and civic obligations in order to maintain a well-run society. It is correct to conceive of the third element of citizenship as two separate elements in its own respect, as there are two types of obligations; both of which, each citizen must fulfill if society hopes to prevent government encroachment. Unfortunately, it must be admitted that we have neglected our obligations, and indeed, progressivism encourages us to do so. *Constitutional obligation* is the duty of a citizen to exercise their rights of protection when necessary. Informed and accountable voting, serving in public office when fit, petitioning the government, and even the bearing of arms if need be, are all civic duties that fulfill our constitutional obligation. This is a citizen-to-government relationship in which the governed either consents or dissents to the actions of the State. When arguing for the need to adopt a Bill of Rights, Patrick Henry understood that to have "implied rights," or what I have referred to as rights of protection, would be unable to combat "implied powers" unless citizens were readily willing to exercise them. Without a society able and willing to exercise their rights of protection, there is little incentive for government to respect individual sovereignty. Government overreach is expected and deserved when the people care little to participate in their political process. But this is not the sum total cause for the state of our union. Certainly there are low information voters, low participation election cycles, and a lack of mobilization in defense of civil rights in some instances. However, there exists a dedicated group of political participants, both individual and assembled, who participate in the political process under a false assumption. Political leaders are obligated to uphold their oath of office, yet we have allowed the lines to become blurred between respecting the office and respecting the individual. Related to this obfuscation is a genuine and justified fear of crossing the line into treason instead of defending the Constitution, which of course, is a direct consequence of a failure to understand Natural Law. There is no oath of allegiance to a man or woman who may hold office in our legislatures, the Office of President or any other position within any other level of government; there is only the Oath of Allegiance to the Constitution, and officeholders are sworn to obey, not defy it:

"I do solemnly swear (or affirm) that I will support and defend the Constitution of the United States against all enemies, foreign and domestic; that I will bear true faith and

allegiance to the same; that I take this obligation freely, without any mental reservation or purpose of evasion; and that I will well and faithfully discharge the duties of the office on which I am about to enter. [So help me God.]. "[81]

Leaders, after all, are government animals who cannot be trusted, even if we hold them in the highest esteem and regard. As often as we overlook how truly meaningless the oath our leaders take has become in their minds, we equally overlook our own failures to hold them accountable. When our leaders impose legislation in opposition to the Natural, or True Law, it is a threat to our liberty and if we are deserving of said liberty it should be rendered invalid by whatever means. No longer do *We the People* understand that we are obliged to obey the Natural Law – as our Founders did – when it required them "to throw off such Government, and to provide new Guards for their future security."[82] If government has been allowed to become oppressive, then it has not been the result of government action *per se*. The forfeiture of our duties is a violation of the True Law, leaving us undeserving of the rights that accompany the "gift of Heaven" – freedom:

"On the contrary, no human legislature has power to abridge or destroy them, unless the owner shall himself commit some act that amounts to a forfeiture."[83]

Societal obligation is a citizen-to-citizen relationship based on an individual's ties to their family, neighborhood, community and nation. Individuals should, and in fact must, care enough about their fellow-citizens to render them affection and assist their empowerment when needed, because the more individuals prosper, the happier society as a whole will become. We established in the prior section that this natural desire exists, but how we choose to meet our needs can mean the difference between liberty and tyranny. The natural tendency of government is to oppress, and it will exploit our needs with the false promise to relieve our unalienable burdens. Armed with an argument grounded in what is "necessary and proper," we can be certain "the wicked will continuously be watching" because it is an unfortunate truth that when we hold government positions "it is in the nature of mankind to be tyrannical."[84] Despots have used emotional arguments to appeal to our basic needs, which of course, always have a

---

[81] 5 U.S.C. § 3331, Oath of Office.

[82] *Declaration of Independence,* 1776. Quoted from Brown, Richard D. *Major Problems in the Era of the American Revolution 1760 – 1791* 2nd Edition, pg. 170 University of Connecticut 2000

[83] Blackstone, William. Commentaries on the Laws of England. Edited by William Carey Jones. Vol. 1 pg. 93 San Francisco: Bancroft – Whitney Co., 1916

[84] Elliot, Jonathan. Patrick Henry speech in the Virginia Convention. *The Debates in the Several State Conventions, on the Adoption of the Federal Constitution, as Recommended by the General Convention at Philadelphia, in1787.* Vol. 4 pg. 148 – 149, 164 – 165 Philadelphia, J.B. Lippincott & co.; Washington, Taylor & Maury, 1836-59.

softly dismissive undertone; as if to say it is a fringe and ridiculous paranoia to fear government solutions. When we compare the words of Alexander Hamilton to those of modern progressives, we find little difference in their tone and intent. Hamilton, who we will discuss further in the following section, deployed the same arguments against the Bill of Rights that progressives have used to propose more "necessary and proper" government intrusion:

"Where in the name of common sense are our fears to end if we may not trust our sons, our brother, our neighbours, our fellow citizen? What shadow of danger can there be from men who are daily mingling with the rest of their countrymen and who participate with them in the same feelings; sentiments, habits, and interest?...In reading many of the publications against the Constitution a man is apt to imagine that he is pursuing some ill written tale or romance which, instead of natural and agreeable images, exhibits to the mind nothing but frightful and distorted shapes – gorgons, hydras, and chimeras dire..."[85]

Modern progressives echo Hamilton's message, which is that we all have in common the belonging of government, and because of this similarity it is mere paranoia to suspect our leaders of ill-intent. This idea, naturally, did not prevail during the Constitutional Convention, as Hamilton was on the fringe in his belief. The consensus, even among other Federalists, was on the idea that government belonged to *We the People*, and not the other way around; healthy amounts of distrust, skepticism and fear of government was natural. We can observe the same political narrative in the Progressive Movement, which survives today, or the idea that conservatives are somehow inferior in their intellect, because there is no "common sense" in this fear. However, American liberty is the exception to history, and despotism is the norm. In his own respect, Patrick Henry also was on the fringe of the debate, as he mistrusted human nature and our ability to sustain virtue. It was a general agreement that the size of the new nation, as it relates to the dangers of failing to sustain sufficient virtue, was of serious concern to our Founding Fathers. Although in America "the moral qualities of the people made the creation of republics peculiarly feasible," the realities of human nature dictated "the larger the state the greater the danger."[86]

At the core of republicanism is the belief that society can draw on the tightness of human relationships to ensure citizens feel obliged to show each other the highest acts of affections. The closer the relationship, then the stronger the obligation to respond to the needs of others is impressed upon us. It pains us to see injustices in the lives of those we care about, and indeed, despair from the suffering of others we are not even intimately familiar with, is common. "For

---

[85] Hamilton, Alexander. *The Federalist* No. 26. *The Federalist Papers.* pg. 168 Edited by Garry Wills. New York: Banthan Dell, 2003

[86] Bailyn, Bernard. *The Ideological Origins of the American Revolution.* pg. 281 Cambridge, MA: Belknap of Harvard University Press, 1992

these virtues originate in our natural inclination to love our fellow-men, and this is the foundation of justice," wrote Cicero of the "True Law," or "right reason in agreement with nature;" of which, our obligation is clear:

"We cannot be freed from its obligations by senate or people, and we need not look outside ourselves for an expounder or interpreter of it."[87]

In other words, we know from our human nature that it is unnatural to defer our obligations to the government. Therefore, if individuals in society wish to enjoy their God-given unalienable rights, as is our natural desire, then we must fulfill our unalienable duties, as well. There is no right that the Laws of Nature and Nature's God have not assigned an equivalent duty or obligation, or as Jefferson phrased it, a citizen "has no right in opposition to his social duties."[88]

It is logical, practical, and in accordance with Natural Law to conclude that dereliction of civic duty – in large part – is responsible for the growth of government and loss of liberty. Whether out of disinterest, or as Peck argued – that it is in our darker nature to avoid our problems – the unnatural deference to the State for basic needs exposes society to the wickedness of despots. A free society in which individuals do not fulfill their civic obligations will soon find they must surrender to the State an unforeseeable portion of their personhood in order to ensure the general public welfare. There will always be citizens who are deficient in fulfilling their basic needs and those in government willing to promise their needs will be met, which is why "only a virtuous people are capable of freedom. As nations become corrupt and vicious, they have more need of masters."[89] We expect to enjoy all of the rights afforded from full citizenship, but we no longer possess the tightness of relationships that renders government action unnecessary and improper. Natural Law commands no deference of our duties. Progressives are successful at creating, exposing, and exploiting areas in which social duties are deferred to government.

Indeed, this has been the cause of the slow but steady degradation of individual sovereignty in American society. Unfortunately, it is motivated by a desire to expand government power, not a genuine desire to meet our citizens' hierarchy of needs. For the past century, at least, federal legislation has been disproportionately passed to promote the progressive domestic agenda. We are meant to believe that one more program, one more tax, or one more piece of our personhood is imperative so that they can attend to the needs of other

---

[87] Quoted from *Great Political Thinkers*. Ebenstein, William. pg. 133, 134 New York: Holt. Reinhart, and Winston, 1963

[88] Jefferson, Thomas. *The Writing of Thomas Jefferson*. Edited by Albert Ellery Bergh. Vol. 16 pg. 282 Washington D.C.: The Thomas Jefferson Memorial Association, 1907

[89] Franklin, Benjamin. *The Writings of Benjamin Franklin*. Edited by Albert Henry Smyth. Vol. 9 pg. 569 New York: The Macmillan Co., 1905 – 1907

citizens. If public happiness is the goal, then we should expect to see a favorable national condition, or evidence of policy success comparative to the forfeited amount of individual liberty. However, as this discussion will expose in the chapters and sections to come, this is evidently not the case. By any measure of health or well-being, economic freedom, general liberty and opportunity for prosperity, the progressive policies of big government have not delivered on their promises. Furthermore, they have only created a greater disparity among our citizens, and worse, impede efforts to rebuild civil society.

There are two needs that are repeatedly exploited for purposes of proposing more "necessary and proper" government action, which has led to excessive government growth, threatening our individual liberty. Basic financial needs and personal safety, historically speaking, have proven to be the greatest areas of vulnerability for our society. Although it may seem that these are two unrelated issues, an examination of why it is "necessary and proper" for government action to meet them reveals they are unquestionably interconnected. Aside from exploiting humankind's basic primal fears, the relationship between poverty and violence – each contributing to the cause of each other – has been well established. Thus far, however, the evidence does not support a conclusion that government action can be successful at combating either. In fact, the conservative countervailing narrative claims that government-centered solutions, at the very least, exacerbate these issues. The empirical evidence, however convincing, cannot be solely relied upon to support the conservative narrative. Apart from the obvious shortcomings of empirical evidence, such as our bias-driven temptation to cherry-pick, raw data fails to capture the depth of our societal problems. Historical data must be coupled with logic and real world common sense to solve real world problems.

The current state of our union is nothing less than the "a wretched situation" that Madison feared we would become "without any virtue in the people," and a Constitution reflecting our values. But the Constitution was adopted and subsequently ratified, yet our modern society has become so wanting of both public and private virtue that federal expenditures to care for the needs of our citizens have produced a national debt that exceeds our entire economy's gross domestic product.[90] Economist Milton Friedman correctly defined the national debt as the amount equal to the future tax bill, which eventually *We the People* must come to satisfy. In 2011 alone, federal, state, and local expenditures on all 126 government assistance programs totaled in excess of $952 billion dollars.[91] Essentially, society is using government as an incredibly expensive and ineffective middle man to perform our societal obligations. Due to the inverted relationship

---

[90] Quote by Madison, James. *The Debates in the Several State Conventions on the Adoption on the Federal Constitution.* Eliot, Jonathon ed. Vol. 3 pg. 536 Philadelphia: J.B. Lippincott Company, 1901
[91] Tanner, Michael. *The American Welfare State: How we Spend Nearly $1 Trillion a Year Fighting Poverty – and Fail.* Policy Analysis 694 pg. 2 Washington D.C.: Cato Institute, 2011

between taxes and freedom, eventually, this will result in a complete loss of liberty and the freedom of self-determination, as we know it. How did this come to pass?

In the following chapter, we will discuss the relatively unknown history of the Progressive Movement, which has inevitably led to the expanded role that government currently plays in American society. The subsequent chapter will be concerned with the role that virtue was intended to play in civil society and explore this as an alternative to government-centered solutions. We will examine the measures our Founding Fathers adopted, which they hoped would sustain virtue, such as the preservation of religion, morality and a strong family composition. Two of our societies' greatest injustices – poverty and violence – illustrate why government, by its nature, is diametrically opposed to the original design alternative and far less effective. The final chapter deals with the need to have and win an honest political discussion, the true nature of government, the choice between society-centered solutions or government-centered solutions, and what the consequences of our choice will mean to the future security of subsequent generations. In essence, I will force America to choose what kind of people we want to be, who we want our children to be, how we want them to live, and if we are strong enough to become worthy to receive credit for the ultimate survival of our once virtuous republic.

CHAPTER 2: PROGRESS OVER VIRTUE

"Is there no virtue among us? If there be not, we are in a wretched situation. No theoretical checks, no form of government, can render us secure. To suppose that any form of government will secure liberty or happiness without any virtue in the people, is a chimerical idea."[1]

James Madison

THE CONTRACT IS BROKEN

Being of central relevance to this discussion, it is worth restating that my thesis rejects prior conservative arguments. The tendency from the right is to focus on the expansion of government as both the initial violation of our social contract, as well as the root cause of our current condition. The correlation might be clear anecdotally, but the argument is underdeveloped. In it's present state, this is an oversimplified copout that runs counter to the history of the Progressive Movement in the United States. During times of greater than normal socio-economic inequality, ideologies that promote "fairness" become attractive propositions to those on the lower end of the economic spectrum. It is certainly true that our Founding Fathers would have found economic programs unconstitutional and even evil for their promotion of idleness, but the amount of leisure time spent in place of philanthropy would have been equally repugnant.[2]

Domestic policy, or at least a general agenda, must secure political support before policy can be implemented into law. There is no doubt we face enormous challenges that are the byproducts of progressive policies. Debt driven by unsustainable entitlements, unfunded union pension liabilities, and chronic high unemployment now threaten our personal and economic sovereignty. But the policies themselves were once a proposed solution to legitimate political issues, such as poverty and unreasonable workplace conditions. Progressive politicians offered social-economic stability in return for public favor, or political support. Socio-cultural deficiencies prevented private solutions, recourse, and reprieve from citizen hardship. This should not have been the case had we not abandoned our founding ideals. Between the absence of another alternative, and the prohibition of education that highlights the dangers of progressivism, it is only logical that these policies soon obtained the support of the American people. For limited government to remain limited, there must be a limited necessity for government intervention.

---

[1] Quoted in *The Debates in the Several State Conventions on the Adoption of the Federal Constitution*. Vol. 3 pgs. 356-357. Philadelphia: J.B. Lippincott Co., 1901

[2] Quoting Franklin and Wesley by Weber, Max. *The Protestant Ethic and Spirit of Capitalism*. pg. 119, 121 New York: Rutledge Publishing, 1992

Modern historians have yet to make a compelling argument that identifies the psychological transition from a society of economic mobility to perceived limited mobility, and inequality. This perception is the soil in which the roots of progressivism took hold. Barbara C. Smith argued that social inequality was cemented in our society immediately after the Revolution:

"In the aftermath of the Revolution, with the coming of the Jacksonian age, Americans faced the limits of human virtue, dismissed their utopian ideals, and accepted the invisible hand of self-interest as their basis for social and political life."[3]

Aside from an improper attempt to reference, or take a cheap shot at Adam Smith, she seems to have erased an entire movement from American history because it stands in contrast to her argument. I concede she has poetic talent in making her point, but her characterization is contradictory to the first hand account of Alexis de Tocqueville. Tocqueville, who was dispatched by the French monarchy to identify the reason for American success described virtue, morality, religion, and strong family composition as the bulwarks of American freedom and economic prosperity. Tocqueville wrote:

"On my arrival in the United State the religious aspect of the country was the first thing that struck my attention; and the longer I stayed there, the more I perceived the great political consequences resulting from this new state of things."[4]

The movement known as the Second Great Awakening, sparked a revival of religious principles and societal virtue, which began in the 1820s. Basically, this activism occurred at the exact time Smith claims we "faced the limits of human virtue."[5] Discussed further in the following chapter, the Second Great Awakening was the driving force behind abolition, early women's suffrage movements, and nurtured those who put us on a path to Gettysburg and Seneca Falls. The period Smith highlights, would more correctly be described as one in which virtue and morality began to demand that all those who had been excluded from full citizenship now realize the Revolution's promise of liberty, and equality. Clearly, as is always the case, there were strong countervailing forces at work with despotic motives.

Due to the efforts of Alexander Hamilton, and other "High Federalists," what was cemented at the founding of our country was the enduring battle between

---

[3] Smith, Barbara Clark. *The Revolution Preserved Social Inequality.* The William and Mary Quarterly, 3rd Series Vol. L1, Number 4, pg. 2 Oct. 1994

[4] Tocqueville, Alexis de. *Democracy in America,* 1840. Vol. 1 pg. 319 New York: Vintage Books, 1945

[5] Smith, Barbara Clark. *The Revolution Preserved Social Inequality.* The William and Mary Quarterly, 3rd Series Vol. L1, Number 4, pg. 2 Oct. 1994

limited government and tyrannical government.[6] In modern interpretations, progressive historians have come to appreciate Hamilton's influence in the early administrations of Washington and Adams. Sean Wilentz, a Princeton scholar, outlines how progressive revisionists in academia praise Hamilton and admonish Jefferson:

"In recent years, Hamilton and his reputation have decidedly gained the initiative among scholars who portray him as the visionary architect of the modern liberal capitalist economy and of a dynamic federal government headed by an energetic executive. Jefferson and his allies, by contrast, have come across as naïve, dreamy idealists. At best according to many historians, the Jeffersonians were reactionary utopians who resisted the onrush of capitalist modernity in hopes of turning America into a yeoman farmers' arcadia. At worst, they were proslavery racists who wish to rid the West of Indians, expand the empire of slavery, and keep political power in local hands — all the better to expand the institution of slavery and protect slaveholders' rights to own human property."[7]

This is a despicable depiction of the political dynamic, which ensued as a result of the competing visions of Hamilton and Jefferson during the early years of our republic. This interpretation paints a historical image unworthy of scholastic consideration, nevertheless, it is useful at exposing their methods of deception. The waving of a shiny object meant to distract the reader, in this case slavery, draws attention away from what they want to remain undiscovered. It is true that Hamilton was an early abolitionist, but so were Thomas Jefferson, Benjamin Franklin, and many other slave-owning Founding Fathers. There are two major contributions from Hamilton that continue to be consequential in our lives today. First, the "capitalist modernity" that Jefferson and the likeminded resisted, was Hamilton's feverous support of government intervention in the economy in favor of businesses deemed necessary by the government, or corporatism. Today, we call this cronyism, and it has resulted in a tremendous amount of special interest corruption, manufactured market failure, and greater economic disparity. But that was the preferred ideology for Hamilton, who was never confident with self-governance, or republicanism. He believed that "the rich and well-born" should be given a "permanent share of government" with a supreme authoritative role over the people.[8] Through his broad interpretation of what was "necessary and proper," which sadly the Supreme Court later affirmed, he justified the need for a

---

[6] Reference to extremists who favored monarchy and opposed republicanism. Federalists such as Adams, favored a strong federal government but, within a republic.

[7] Sean Wilentz, Review of *Empire of Liberty: a History of the Early Republic, 1789 – 1815. Journal of American History* Sept, 2010 Vol. 97 #2 pg. 476

[8] *Notes of the Secret Debates of the Federal Convention*, 1787. Taken by the Late Hon Robert Yates, Chief Justice of the State of New York, and One of the Delegates from That State to the Said Convention."

National Bank that would allow him to push wealth-producing policy for his elitist friends. At the expense of the poor's misfortunes, Hamilton made his High Federalist friends very wealthy. Senator William Maclay, recorded in his journal the unscrupulous events that took place:

"Hamilton, at the head of the speculators, with all the courtiers, are on one side. These I call the party who are actuated by interest."[9]

The amendment put forward for debate that Senator Maclay was addressing, which Madison unsuccessfully opposed, allowed for speculators to assume the same interest as the original debt holder. Jefferson described the result as:

"twenty millions of stock divided among favored States, and thrown in as pabulum to the stock-jobbing herd, . . ."[10]

These original debt holders were individual citizens, dispersed throughout all states, whom had pledged their fortunes to the cause of the Revolutionary War. Yet, when Madison tried to amend the measure with a modest suggestion to impose fair discrimination on the speculators, Hamilton ensured it was defeated. Hamilton's practices provided a template for later progressive politicians to use their corrupt business relationships to funnel wealth away from the highly autonomous agrarian economies, and concentrate as much as possible in the North. The idea that slavery had a prominent bearing on their motives, which were wealth and power, is patently false. Wealth and market control gave them the ability to make unaccountable predatory loans on "free" minorities, and manufacture crisis so they could propose "necessary" government intervention in the private sector. The real goal was to wrestle powers away from *We the People* and our individual states, which were inconveniently protected under our Constitution. Although the issues may change, within modern American politics the tactics, promises and intentions remain the same, nonetheless.

The second consequential contribution arose out of opposition to Hamilton's financial legislative agenda. Madison, together with Virginia Congressman William Branch Giles, established a Congressional caucus to organize opposition to Hamilton's proposals. Upon his return from France, Jefferson joined the coalition and together they argued against establishing the Bank of the United States. The emergence of the Republican Party, whom historians have deemed Democratic-Republicans, marked the beginning of party dominance in American politics. There had always been Federalists and Anti-Federalists, but the spirit of

[9] Maclay, William. *Journal of William Maclay, United States Senator from Pennsylvania, 1789–1791.* Edited by Edgar S. Maclay pg. 197 New York: D. Appleton & Co., 1890
[10] Jefferson, Thomas. *The Writings of Thomas Jefferson.* Vol. 1 pg. 270 Edited by Albert Ellery Bergh. Washington D.C.: Thomas Jefferson Memorial Association, 1903

cooperation that had been marveled at by the Founding Fathers during the Constitutional Convention, had evaporated; leaving behind bitter partisan political discourse. The existence of organized political parties in American politics, which Washington warned us not to establish, arose in large part from one individual's meddling ambition. John Adams, a member of the Federalist party no less, had thought Hamilton to be unprincipled, overly ambitious and exhibited dangerous aristocratic tendencies. In fact, there is a good deal of evidence to suggest that had Adams not fired his cabinet, then Hamilton might have carried out a monarchal coup d'état as Adams had suspected. After his antics during the election of 1800, Hamilton influence was finished with the Federalist party as far as Congress was concerned.[11] In 1802, after threatening to leave the Federalist Party he had so-fractured, Hamilton established The Christian Constitutional Society. Of course, this was nothing more than another angle aimed at exerting lost political influence. Following his affair with Marie Reynolds, and subsequent blackmail by her husband that became public knowledge, his continuously flawed reputation made him highly suspect of any virtuous undertaking.[12] The organization stressed the superiority of Christian principles, even over our Constitution.[13] Hamilton never got the chance, however, after he organized the defeat of the Federalist candidate for New York's gubernatorial election – Aaron Burr. Although Hamilton died in 1804, no bullet could kill his legacy that lived on throughout the Gilded Age, the culture within the Treasury Department, and progressive economic intervention that has dominated American policy since 1861.[14]

Government involvement at the federal level, or centralization, increased dramatically in the second half of the 19th century. The recent challenge to the consensus that holds the westward expansion of slavery as a predominant cause of the Civil War is a completely warranted challenge, however, best left for another examination. For the purposes of this chapter, more concern will be given to whether or not the federal expansion of power over states' rights was as effective in providing equal rights and lessening corruption at the state level, as we all have been led to believe. What can be said for sure is that westward expansion, and later the Civil War, strained and disrupted the foundations of society that are the breeding grounds for virtue – the family and community.

Prior to the war, mechanization had already begun to demand young, often too young, able-bodied workers at the expense of any deference to the elderly.

[11] Elkins, Stanley, & McKitrick Eric. *The Age of Federalism.* New York: Oxford University Press, 1993

[12] Schachner, Nathan. *Alexander Hamilton.* pg. 368 New York: D. Appleton Century Company. 1946.

[13] West, John G. and MacLean, S. *The Encyclopedia of Religion in American Politics.* Greenwood Publishing, 1999

[14] Lind, Michael. *Hamilton's Republic: Readings in the American Democratic Nationalist Tradition.* New York: Free, 1997

Railroads and other businesses plowing westward ensured competition for employment was fierce, pitting young against old for employment opportunities. Industry justified poor workplace conditions, low wages, the reneging of pension promises and other shoddy business practices, by claiming it was necessary to compete with free labor production in the South. As was previously alluded to, the manufactured historical record paints a picture of a progressive North embracing the future, while in reality, workplace conditions were comparable to the evil institution of slavery. Sure, industrial workers were free to leave in theory, but it is a long walk to nowhere when you are filthy, tired, and your stomach is empty. This chapter in American history has received some valid criticism. However, the Progressive Era has been the beneficiary of unwarranted praise at the expense of Adam Smith, and consequentially capitalism. Adam Smith's version of capitalism never condoned such selfish civic recklessness, nor did our Founders' interpretations of it. Furthermore, neither was the relationship between the government and private business ever intended to become so entangled. Special interest, or what Adam Smith referred to as factions, were never permitted to establish guilds, monopolies, or outright oligarchies. This is another false mantra that has blossomed out of the progressive narrative. Smith was adamantly opposed to such concentrations of economic power, and even more so, the establishment of a corrupt relationship between business and government. In Smith's own words:

"People of the same trade seldom meet together, even for merriment and diversion, but the conversation ends in a conspiracy against the public, or in some contrivance to raise prices. It is impossible indeed to prevent such meetings, by any law which either could be executed, or would be consistent with liberty and justice. But though the law cannot hinder people of the same trade from sometimes assembling together, it ought to do nothing to facilitate such assemblies; much less to render them necessary."[15]

The modern understanding of capitalism, which tends to focuses on greed or the accumulation of wealth for wealth's sake, would be totally unrecognizable to our Founding Fathers – or even the early-mid 19th century American. Factions existed in colonial America to a certain extent, but they did not tear the political and economical order apart, and they abided by established rules barring against violence and excess.[16] The centralization of wealth occurred along a parallel timeline with the centralization of government. The amount of cronyism that began to develop between progressive industry and politicians in the late 19th century produced what is now the unrivaled level Washington D.C. engages in

[15] Smith, Adam. *An Inquiry into the Nature and Causes of The Wealth of Nations.* Vol. 1 pg. 80 DigiReads Publishing, 2009
[16] Middlekauff, Robert. *The Glorious Cause: The American Revolution, 1763 – 1789* Revised & Expanded Edition. pg. 45 Oxford University Press 2005

today. Max Weber, the German sociologist and political economist, wrote of the origins, history, and "spirit" of true capitalism:

"The impulse to acquisition, pursuit of gain, of money, of the greatest possible amount of money, has in itself nothing to do with capitalism. This impulse exists and has existed among waiters, physicians, coachmen, artists, prostitutes, dishonest officials, soldiers, nobles, crusaders, gamblers, and beggars. One may say that it has been common to all sorts and conditions of men at all times and in all countries of the earth, wherever the objective possibility of it is or has been given. It should be taught in the kindergarten of cultural history that this naïve idea of capitalism must be given up once and for all. Unlimited greed for gain is not in the least identical with capitalism, and is still less its spirit."[17]

The entire progressive argument and, indeed, the ideological premise of modern collectivism, relies on a non-existent, self-created straw man. The hybrid interventionalist liberal economy that manufactures unnatural markets, which naturally fail to crisis, barely resembles classical American capitalism. Not only did Adam Smith oppose special interest relationships, price fixing, gouging, and so on, he was skeptical of the effectiveness of regulation to prevent such activity. Smith, there can be little doubt, would contend that cronyism is preventing the market's ability to render the practice of greed undesirable for business. Government subsidies, and subsequent price fixing, creates market conditions where it becomes virtually impossible for any producer outside of established political circles to compete and gain a competitive advantage. The American economy is, and has been for some time, a type of hologram capitalism. That is to say, the image of what we know to be capitalism is not at all what is in front of us when we participate in markets. Instead of ensuring market conditions are consistent for all participants, or as popularly coined "everybody plays by the same rules," in reality government has exacerbated disparity. Market failures "come about not in spite of our efforts at improving market design, but because of them."[18] Washington outlined what he believed the proper role of the government should be in a free market:

"Let vigorous measures be adopted; not to limit the price of articles, for this I believe is inconsistent with the very nature of things, and impractical in itself, but to punish speculators, forestallers, and extortioners, and above all to sink the money by heavy taxes. To promote public and private economy; encourage manufacturers, ..."[19]

---

[17] *Introduction.* Weber, Max. *The Protestant Ethic and Spirit of Capitalism.* XXXi New York: Rutledge Publishing, 1992

[18] Bookstaber, Richard. *A Demon of our own Design: Markets, Hedge Funds, and the Perils of Financial Innovation.* pg. 5 NJ: John Wiley and Sons, 2007

[19] Washington, George. *The Writing of George Washington.* Edited by John C. Fitzpatrick. Vol. 14 pg. 313 Washington: United States Government Printing Office, 1931 – 1944

Progressive politicians certainly encouraged manufacturers in industrial states, but they favored using government to manipulate the market in a manner that is discouraged by the economic philosophy of Smith, and our Founders. Although it is not my aim to defame President Lincoln, who most assuredly deserves reverence for his wartime wisdom, his administration contained statist elements. President Lincoln, who is ironically celebrated alongside Washington in popular culture, did not agree with respect to taxation. Treasury Secretary Salmon P. Chase, was the first to impose a progressive income tax in 1862. By 1864, taxes on annual incomes between $600 to $5,000 increased to 5 percent, from the original 3 percent tax on incomes up to $10,000. Accordingly, a 7.5 percent tax was levied on income between $5,000 - $10,000, and 10 percent on incomes over $10,000. The law was again amended a meager year later, which imposed a 10 percent tax on all annual incomes over $5,000.[20] At the close of the war, concern surrounding taxation induced inflation and whether or not the federal government even needed the revenue anymore, commenced. On March 2nd 1867, after considerable debate, Congress settled on a 5 percent flat tax on all annual incomes over $1,000. Excuse after excuse from the federal government to raise, and subsequently make permanent a temporary measure, soon made clear their intentions to secure a permanent federal tax authority.

What began as an effort to support the war, evolved into the now familiar class warfare rhetoric as opposition mounted. While precise figures were scarcely known to the public at large, during the decade the war tax was implemented it amounted to $346 million in revenue. Out of which, only $55 million in revenues were collected during wartime when Lincoln's cabinet argued a tax necessity. The remaining burden was assumed through debt that was in excess of $2.5 billion.[21] One might logically question what the true intention of the war tax was in the first place. What were widely understood, however, were the realities of income taxation. Though the flat tax had been seen as a more "fair" measure than the previous progressive tax structure, the burden fell unduly on the lower-class taxpayer. Even Mark Twain took to his satirical pen to describe the lack of disconcert among the elitist class. In *A Mysterious Visit*, an article widely circulated during the 1870s, Twain tells a story of how he unknowingly boasts to a tax collector, who upon discovery of Twain's $214,000 annual income, promptly hands him paperwork to file. James Ford Rhoads retells the tale as written by Twain:

"In despair he went for advice to an acquaintance, an opulent man who lived in a palace

---

[20] Seligman, Edwin R. *Theory, and Practice of Income Taxation at Home and Abroad.* pg. 67 New York: Macmillan Co., 1911

[21] James G. Randall, *The Civil War and Reconstruction.* 16 United States Statue at Large 256. Chp. 18 Boston, MA: Heath, 1937

and paid no income tax, and he was told how he might make himself out a pauper 'by deftly manipulating the bill of Deductions.' The opulent man took up his pen and set down his 'Losses by shipwreck, fire,' etc. at so much; 'losses on sales of real estate,' on 'live stock sold,' on 'repairs, improvements, interest,' etc., etc., at so much more. 'He got astonishing deductions out of each and every one of these matters,' writes Mark Twain; 'and when he was done he handed me the paper and I saw at a glance that during the year my income in the way of profits had been $1250.40.'...'Now,' said the opulent man, 'the thousand dollars is exempt by law. What you want to do is to go and swear this document in and pay tax on the two hundred and fifty dollars.' 'Do you,' said I, 'do you always work up the deductions after this fashion in your own case sir?' "Well, I should say so! If it weren't for those eleven saving clauses under the head of Deductions, I should be beggared every year to support this hateful and wicked, this extortionate and tyrannical government.'"[22]

The public, being generally skeptical of federal power during this period, grew hostile once again toward income taxation in any form. During the market reverberations caused after the financial panic of 1873, efforts to propose income tax measures were seen by the public as the crisis exploitations they were. Government manipulations of the economy, including annual tax proposals, have been incessant since this period. Politicians would have to find a way to ratify a constitutional amendment to carry out future reforms of such magnitude. The means to achieve these reforms would have long-term effects on our economy, our Constitution, and our social contract. Perhaps, the most consequential example regarding our current challenges, was the manipulation of the market's most precious capital – labor. The political climate in America – both during and post Reconstruction – made this a not-so daunting challenge.

During Reconstruction it became clear that the Northern victory succeeded in the preservation of the Union, but at a great cost to societal unity. As large-scale war too often does, many families and communities were displaced, losing generations of wealth and property. The increased industrialization of the American economy, and labor's interests, threatened the financial stability of elderly family members. Indeed, in great part due to the progressive propaganda campaign to be discussed in the following section, many of those needs were not met. Robert H. Ziegler, a public policy scholar whom I was privy to study under, detailed the economic realities and effectiveness of their efforts:

"As the pace of mechanization accelerated, older workers, employers and pundits agreed, could not keep up. And as the young moved to the cities, families nucleated, leaving no rooms, for the superannuated parents or grandparents."[23]

---

[22] Rhoades, James F. *History of the United States from the Compromise of 1850.* Vol. 6 pg. 393 – 394 New York: Macmillan Co., 1906

[23] Zieger, R.H. *The Development of Federal Old – Age Policy in the Era of the Great Depression: Pensions, Policies, and Politics 1920 – 1940.* Journal of Aging, Humanities, and the Arts pg. 252 July 1ˢᵗ 2008

The psychological transformation of our representative republic to a perceived democracy was not an accident. It was the product of the self-serving interests of politicians and special interest. With respect to labor, they developed relationships that might have appeared to be in conflict, yet in reality were mutually beneficial. Throughout the final three decades of the 19th century, an unnatural transformation of the white middle class workforce was underway. A younger workforce, despite some drawbacks, was a win-win situation for politicians and industry. Productivity increased and promises of old-age insurance from the government provided political stability to those who would support pension reforms. Perceptions of the elderly turned increasingly negative as politicians tapped media sympathizers, academic elites and pension critics, to engage in propaganda smear campaigns.[24] The following section will cover this undertaking, the countervailing narrative and why it lost, the real origin of pension schemes, and some of the short and long-term damages they have had on our society.

The history of the Progressive Era suggests a nudged response to rugged individualism without virtue gone awry. That is to say, the public was constantly nudged ever-so slightly in the direction of big government and less freedom. As civic virtue in our society began to wane, big government and special interest power centers raced to fill the void. By the time the repeated manufactured crises had arrived, the political players and their plans had already been in place, ready to be forced onto a softened public. The result was the exploitation, not further inclusion, of older white middle class workers, Native Americans, black Americans, other minority groups, and an unprecedented expansion in the role of government. Whatever the events, logic or reason, the American social contract as our Founding Fathers understood it, had been broken.

THE BIRTH OF BIG GOVERNMENT CRONYISM & DEMOCRATIC DESPOTISM

Political debate on government assistance programs exists within a false narrative pushed by the progressive left, and remains relatively unchallenged by the right. The emphasis on New Deal reforms, such as the Social Security Act of 1935, insinuates a Depression-induced need for government assistance during a time of market failure in the first half of the 20th century. This allows the left to employ tactics that ally their ideology with the working and middle class members of the electorate. Following the financial crisis in 2008, the progressive

---

[24] Achenbaum, W.A. *Old Age in the new Land: The American experience since 1790.* Baltimore MD: Johns Hopkins University Press, 1978

message was effective at justifying excessive government spending and growth by using an incorrect analogy to the market failures prior to the Great Depression. In a more appropriate analogy, as was the case with the New Deal Reforms, the American Recovery and Reinvestment Act of 2009 did not deliver on the promise of broad economic opportunity. Stimulus spending totaling in excess of $800 billion destroyed and delayed at least one million private sector jobs, while funneling money to labor and other political allies through public projects.[25]

The conservative narrative has included a general acceptance of the progressive version of history. They, too, scapegoat the era of the Great Depression, which emphasizes the New Deal reforms. They will not challenge this through a countervailing narrative, because it masks their own neglect and compliance. By breaking free of the constructed history we can identify that socio-economic factors, most of which manufactured, that justified expanding the size and scope of government programs. From this perspective, we can fully appreciate the damage they have done and continue to do to American society. Rather than expand the borders of citizenship, thus increasing opportunity, they have changed the relationship between the individual and the State. For reasons to be explained, this has had an adverse effect on citizenship and traditional American institutions in civil society. Naturally, the results have hindered the ability of individuals to obtain even the most basic elements in their hierarchy of needs. Family composition, as a consequence, continues to suffer and degenerate.

The rise of the soon-to-be broken promise, which is now the modern welfare apparatus in the United States, began with the same characteristics that we see present today – abuse, greed, and corruption. Political cronyism aimed at the transfer of wealth to progressives and their alliances, were constructed under the guise of addressing the economic needs of veterans, the elderly, and labor.[26] The economic and social consequences have proven to be far greater than the benefits. The culture of dependency is but one danger posed to our society from government meddling in affairs, which up until the industrial revolution were traditionally managed by the family and community. These government schemes, however, did not manifest in the aftermath of the Great Depression. As early as Reconstruction, progressive politicians promised pension benefits to soldiers who had fought in the Civil War. Veterans returned to find an increasingly industrious nation in the North in demand of a younger workforce and new skills. In the South, the agrarian economy was adopting their own cost-cutting measures to offset the added expense realized from new labor wages.

The Grand Army of the Republic, or GAR, represents one of the earliest

---

[25] Conley, Timothy; & Dupor, Bill. *The American Recovery and Reinvestment Act: Public Sector Jobs Saved, Private Sector Jobs Forestalled.* University of Western Ontario/Ohio State University Departments of Economics, 2011

[26] Higgs, Robert. *Crisis and Leviathan: Critical Episodes in the Growth of American Government.* pg. 113 – 114 New York: Oxford University Press, 1987

examples of progressive government corruption. Established in 1866, the GAR was a veteran organization that became a lobby to members of Congress willing to provide special interest favors in return for political support. The result of this corrupt partnership was the public funding of pensions that were overwhelmingly distributed to northern residents and black American veterans. Spending on the program ballooned amidst charges of fraud, fiscal recklessness, and influence-peddling. The charges leveled were common sense oriented. At one point, an endorsement from the Grand Army of the Republic was a must for a progressive seeking a nomination. Even in 19th century America the act of paying for votes proved costly. President Grover Cleveland, notorious for his opposition to corruption, vetoed a congressional proposal to further expand eligibilities to veterans and their relatives with disabilities that were non-service connected. Unfortunately, a single presidential veto is not enough to guard the people's money. For a thirty-year period beginning in 1880, Civil War pensions consumed up to 25% of the annual federal budget.[27] Despite the disaster, progressive pension advocate Isaac Rubinow, would later say that the corrupt legislation was "an economic measure which aims to solve the problem of dependent old-age and widowhood."[28]

Progressive policies, as they most often do, sound as if they are admirable responses to legitimate political challenges. However, the GAR lobby and their pension advocate allies in Congress either failed, or didn't care to think through the consequences. Politically speaking it was a nightmare for the pension movement, but the long-term damage to the black American civil rights movement, was grave. Reconstruction was one disaster after another, however, it was an era of black American representation in southern state legislatures, at the very least. Southern politicians and taxpayers, who were forced to pay the tax to fund the pensions, were furious at the exclusion of Confederate veterans.[29] Renewed, or in many cases brand new, hostility toward the North translated into political support for the infamous "Redeemer" governments.[30] They regained control of once-multiracial legislatures in the South, which resulted in waves of legislation passed during the period from 1887 – 1901. These laws laid the foundation for the decades of oppression to be suffered by "free blacks" in the South. Segregation and voting restrictions were legally protected under these reactionary laws, which effectively ushered in what we now refer to as Jim Crow. A scholar, or anyone else, would be hard-pressed to find a better example

[27] Zieger, R.H. *The Development of Federal Old – Age Policy in the Era of the Great Depression: Pensions, Policies, and Politics 1920 – 1940.* Journal of Aging, Humanities, and the Arts pg. 256 July 1st 2008
[28] Quoted in Skocpol, Theda *Social Policy in the United States: Future possibilities in historical perspective.* pg. 71 Princeton, NJ: Princeton University Press 1995
[29] Zieger, R.H. *The Development of Federal Old – Age Policy in the Era of the Great Depression: Pensions, Policies, and Politics 1920 – 1940.* Journal of Aging, Humanities, and the Arts pg. 257 July 1st 2008
[30] Reference to name given to all white male Democrat controlled southern legislatures during and post Reconstruction who sought to rollback civil rights advancements in 19th century.

of progressivism's impact on the law of unintended consequences.

Ironically, progressive politicians would later point to the pension program established for the GAR to advocate the need for more inclusion in future programs. Unfortunately for them, following the GAR debacle, pension reform faced considerable headwinds from state legislatures, governors' vetoes, and members of Congress. The emergence of the countervailing narrative that defended the rights of older workers resulted in considerable pushback. They charged younger workers, and justifiably so, with having high turnover rates, chronic truancy, and a greater susceptibility to activist influence.[31] Public pension reform now had a rival in the proponents of "voluntary collectivism." To be fair, many large corporations and politicians made up this coalition. Even some social science academics began to resist the claims of their colleagues who had neglected to focus on the social stability of the family composition. Study after study was released, of which each contradicted the other, culminating up to the onset of the Great Depression. The messaging war was reminiscent of a theme frequently heard today. The Massachusetts Commission on Old Age Pensions, echoed by the American Way of Life, criticized the European model of a bloated bureaucracy running state-controlled pension plans. The movement praised American corporations, including General Electric and Westinghouse, for voluntarily practicing "welfare capitalism." In reality, the railroad industry had instituted pension plans as early as the 1870s. From 1911 – 1925, there had been close to 400 private industry pension plans consisting of annuities and other insurance products.[32]

Ultimately, the anti-elderly worker narrative proved too much to overcome. Businesses, despite the difficulty inherent from younger workers hired them, nevertheless. Ziegler attributes this outcome to two factors, stating:

"For the most part, however, more negative views prevailed. Personnel managers relied on "common sense" rather than social science in hiring and retention matter."[33]

This certainly speaks to the difficulty of countering a message, especially a populist driven message, once it has been established. The progressive politicians had identified a potential weakness in our society. The family composition's inability to solve the problem of superannuated workers was both manufactured, as will be examined deeper in the following section, and subsequently exploited. Government-run pension programs promised to relieve citizens of their societal

---

[31] Graebner, W. *A History of Retirement: The meaning and function of an American institution, 1885 – 1978* Connecticut: Yale University Press, 1980

[32] Lubove, R. *The Struggle for Social Security.* pg. 127 – 132 Cambridge MA: Harvard University Press, 1968

[33] Zieger, R.H. *The Development of Federal Old – Age Policy in the Era of the Great Depression: Pensions, Policies, and Politics 1920 – 1940.* Journal of Aging, Humanities, and the Arts pg. 253 July 1st 2008

obligations during a period of difficult economic times. There remained, however, significant barriers to progressive reforms.

The Congress remained in opposition to direct federal payments to individuals. Following the GAR program, the states had made it a priority to reign in expenditures by limiting recipients and restricting eligibility. State legislatures had already been under scrutiny from progressive proponents of a constitutional amendment to reform senatorial elections. William Jennings Bryan, and the Populist Party, had been successful in western states campaigning to increase support for popular Senate elections. Bryan, a progressive Democrat, opposed the gold standard while promoting "Free Silver," supported a progressive income tax, and openly objected to a representative republic in favor of popular democracy.[34] Although the Jacksonian Age had done much to advance the "one person one vote" principle, amendment proposals in 1826, 1829, and again in 1855, had all been tabled with no serious consideration. The passage, and subsequent ratification of the 17th Amendment, fundamentally changed the terms of our social contract.

The obvious and most celebrated, with no thought to consequence, was the transformation of our republic into a democratic-republic. The focus on the populous point of view both blindly ignores the amendment's repercussions, and covers hidden intentions that were far more sinister than the text books let on. Progressives argued the need for the amendment was due to the special interest influence on state legislatures, and electoral deadlock. Inexperienced state legislatures in western states, faulting the plurality election system, did fail to send representation on a few occasions. However, representation was no longer an issue by the time the amendment was being seriously considered in the early 20th century. In 1866, a federal law had already been passed requiring state legislatures to elect senators by majority vote and not through plurality as previously practiced. A simple amendment to this statute requiring run-off elections would have eradicated electoral deadlock.[35] The claim that this presented a problem to the proper functionality of government had already been outdated, and discredited. Furthermore, there existed no federal restrictions that would have prevented approaching deadlock with states' rights-centered solutions. The "Oregon Plan," for instance, demonstrated that a federal constitutional amendment was completely unnecessary to address deadlock.[36] The plan required candidates for the state legislature to sign one of two binding statements prior to running for office. One statement pledged to support the

---

[34] Reference to the inflationary monetary policy that advocated abolishing the Gold Standard. Proponents were called "Silverites," who even agreed the cost of goods would increase.

[35] Haynes, George Henry. *The Senate of the United States, Its History and Practice.* New York: Russell & Russell, 1960

[36] Zywicki, Todd J. *Senators and Special Interests: A Public Choice Analysis of the Seventeenth Amendment.* Oregon Law Review Vol. 73 University of Oregon School of Law, 1994

winner of the popular primary vote, while the other reserved the traditional right to vote their conscious. The states' rights-centered solution proved to preserve the people's interest, as a Republican-controlled state legislature sent a Democratic candidate to the Senate after winning the popular primary vote.[37]

David Graham Phillips famously the case against special interest corruption in a nine-part series of articles published in *Cosmopolitan* magazine in 1906, entitled *Treason in the Senate*. An April edition read:

"The combination of bribery and party prejudice is potent everywhere; but there come crises when these fail 'the interests' for the moment…A few thousand dollars put in the experienced hands of the heelers, and the senatorial general agent of 'the interests' is secure for another six years. The Aldrich machine controls the legislature, the election boards, the courts—the entire machinery of the 'republican form of government.' In 1904, when Aldrich needed a legislature to reelect him for his fifth consecutive term, it is estimated that carrying the state cost about two hundred thousand dollars—a small sum, easily to be got back by a few minutes of industrious pocket-picking in Wall Street…The greatest single hold of 'the interests' is the fact that they are the 'campaign contributors'—the men who supply the money for 'keeping the party together,' and for "getting out the vote. Did you ever think where the millions for watchers, spellbinders, halls, processions, posters, pamphlets, that are spent in national, state and local campaigns come from?…there you have in a few words the whole story of the Senate's treason under Aldrich's leadership, and of why property is concentrating in the hands of the few and the little children of the masses are being sent to toil in the darkness of mines, in the dreariness and unhealthfulness of factories instead of being sent to school; and why the great middle class and the old-fashioned Americans, the people with the incomes of from two thousand to fifteen thousand a year—is being swiftly crushed into dependence and the repulsive miseries of 'genteel poverty.'"[38]

The value of the 17th Amendment's ability to stop rampant corruption within the state legislatures, which supposedly worked against the people's interests, is a complete historical myth. Industry and labor had their fair share of corrupt politicians who legislated based on their interests. In fact, prior to *Treason in the Senate*, the first and only two senators who were charged and convicted for violating the 1864 statute, which outlawed the practice of accepting special interest retainer fees among other activities, were both progressives. Joseph Burton of Kansas and Oregon's John Mitchell, were progressive Republicans in the era of Theodore Roosevelt. To Phillips, that would have mattered little, as he was an equal opportunity muckraker. Even Roosevelt, himself, described Phillips

---

[37] Eaton, Allen H. *The Oregon System: The Story of Direct Legislation in Oregon.* pgs. 92 – 98 Chicago: A. C. McClurg, 1912

[38] Quoted from David Graham Phillips, *The Treason of the Senate.* pg. 628 – 638 Cosmopolitan Magazine, April 1906.

as a muckraker with a background resembling "yellow journalism" more than it did "personal journalism."[39] A reasonable conclusion can be made that a good amount of corruption existed prior to the passage of the 17th Amendment. An anticorruption reputation propelled President Cleveland's career in the 1880s, but the empirical evidence demonstrates that the 17th Amendment did more to concentrate special interest in and around the federal government, and created the conditions for their long-term profit. Todd Zywicki, a historian from George Mason University found:

"Empirical tests have demonstrated support for the proposition that the movement from direct elections of senators was an attempt to change the institutional structure in which rent-seeking behavior took place. The Seventeenth Amendment increased the average tenure of senators, thereby making available a greater number of special-interest contracts, as well as increasing their durability and value."[40]

Whether or not popular senatorial elections, as a philosophical matter, are more or less beneficial to the fairness of self-government is debatable. Whether or not proponents of direct elections were honest in their intentions, although I do not believe that to be the case and will prove so, is too debatable. However, the bottom line is that the 17th Amendment did not have the effect that the progressive historical texts have suggested. Moreover, the complete opposite has been the result, which has not served the interest of the American public, but ironically distanced the government further from the people. The data would suggest that, indeed, the people's interest never was the primary consideration, after all.

As demonstrated by Figure 2.1, the average tenure of Senators exploded after the passage and ratification of the 17th amendment. The trend, although not at such a suspicious pace, had been on the increase prior. Previous explanations have included an increase in life expectancy, an ease in traveling due to technological advances, incumbent advantages, and so on.[41] The data does not support the validity of these explanations. A comparable upward trend in tenure within the House of Representatives, does not display similar steep increases at specific periods of time. The value of holding a legislative position, especially in the Senate, increased as the authority of the government increased over the economy. The ability to regulate, or interfere, with the market economy allows the government to transfer wealth to special interest. Following the Civil War,

---

[39] Reference to journalist who used sensationalism, exaggerated, and had little evidence to support the unethical charges. Whereas, personal journalism was a honest citizen watchdog effort.

[40] Zywicki, Todd J. *Senators and Special Interests: A Public Choice Analysis of the Seventeenth Amendment.* pg. 1054 *Oregon Law Review* Vol. 73, University of Oregon School of Law, 1994

[41] John R. Hibbing. *The Modern Congressional Career.* pg. 425 *The American Political Science Review*, Vol. 85, June, 1991

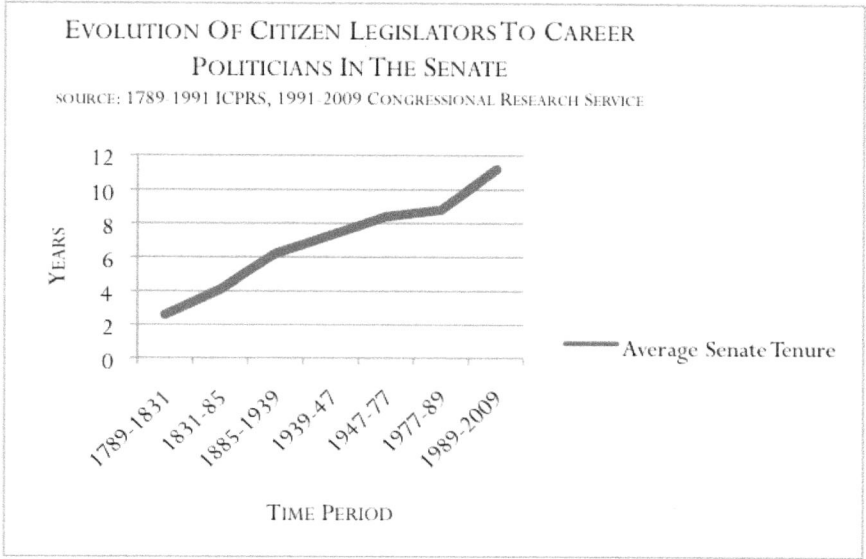

EVOLUTION OF CITIZEN LEGISLATORS TO CAREER
POLITICIANS IN THE SENATE

SOURCE: 1789-1991 ICPRS, 1991-2009 CONGRESSIONAL RESEARCH SERVICE

Figure 2.1: Munn v. Illinois clearly had an impact on tenure, but it was not until the logrolling deal for the 16th & 17th Amendments was the legal authority institutionalized. Only then is the impact on tenure significant, which reflects the 1885-1939 increases to 6-7.5 years. Note the brief New Deal blowback (1939-1947) before increases continue, which is why I blocked periods, in order to control for ideological variances.

institutional changes in Congress, as well as government intent to increase the size and scope of legislative authority did make continued tenure in the Senate more attractive.[42] However, intention alone does not grant authority. Legislators and judicial activists, on the other hand, are frequently the culpable parties.

In *Munn v. Illinois* (1877), the Supreme Court shifted away from precedent and the high court's previous constitutional interpretations, which favored protecting individual property rights over their subservience to the "public" interest.[43] The case revolved around the Illinois legislature's authority, or lack there of, to regulate and set grain storage rates. Munns & Scott, a grain warehouse company, wanted to run their business as every other American business before them – profitably. The Supreme Court interpreted property in such a manner that nearly all private property could be deemed "public" in nature. Authored by Chief Justice Waite, the opinion reads:

"When, therefore, one devotes his property to a use in which the public has an interest, he,

---

[42] H. Douglas Price. *Congress and the Evolution of Legislative Professionalism.* Edited by Norman Ornstein, *Congress in Change.* New York: Praeger Publishers, 1995
[43] Anderson, Terry L. and Hill, Peter J. *The Birth of a Transfer Society.* Stanford, CA: Hoover Institution Press, 1980

in effect, grants to the public an interest in that use, and must submit to be controlled by the public for the common good, to the extent of the interest he has thus created. He may withdraw his grant by discontinuing the use; but, so long as he maintains the use, he must submit to the control.[44]

Justice Fields, prophetically wrote the chilling consequences in his dissent:

"If this be sound law, if there be no protection...all property and all business in the State are held at the mercy of a majority of its legislature. The public has no greater interest in the use of buildings for the storage of grain than it has in the use of buildings for the residences of families...The public is interested in the manufacture of cotton, woolen, and silken fabrics, in the construction of machinery, in the printing and publication of books and periodicals, and in the making of utensils of every variety, useful and ornamental; indeed, there is hardly an enterprise or business engaging the attention and labor of any considerable portion of the community, in which the public has not an interest in the sense in which that term is used by the court in its opinion..."[45]

Munn v. Illinois (1877) legitimized, or condoned, the submission of property owner's rights to the legislature in cases *"in which the public has an interest."*[46] By such a broad interpretation of legitimate legislative power, senators had available a variety of benefits to offer special interest, that is of course, with the powers that derive from tenure seniority. In order to enforce their new authority, Congress established the Interstate Commerce Commission, which became the template for future regulatory agencies. Through regulation, special interest could now purchase a competitive advantage by supporting a legislative candidate. The snag, however, was in the lack of durability for purchased legislation. Regulation, as a whole, does not provide interest groups with a lump-sum return, therefore, the law's durability dictates the value of regulatory legislation.[47] Absent seniority and incumbency, special interest cannot insulate favored laws from reconsideration in a subsequent Congress. As Zywicki very plainly explains:

"If the effectiveness of a legislative act can be guaranteed only until the next electoral session, the value of legislation to interest groups will decline. As a result, these groups will be unwilling to make substantial investments in purchasing legislation that may be obsolete within a few months or years, or which may require investment of further resources at a

---

[44] *Munn v. Illinois*, 94 U.S. 113 (1877).
[45] Ibid.
[46] Ibid.
[47] Posner, Richard A. *Economic Analysis of Law.* 4th ed. Boston, MA: Little, Brown, 1992

later date."[48]

In other words, the increase in the tenure among senators had nothing to do with fair democracy, and everything to do with special interest securing a favored competitive advantage, which produces wealth for the few fortunate who enjoy political connections. *Munn v. Illinois* (1877), and accompanying Granger Cases, sent a signal to special interest that it was open season for cronyism in our representative bodies of government.[49] The best way to ensure the durability of favored special interest legislation is to ensure that the coalition of politicians who support the legislation retain their tenure. There are some in academia who will contend that progressive motives were pure, and continue to perpetuate the aforementioned justifications for careerism in Congress. An examination, however, of the western states' delegations prior to and after the 17th Amendment puts the proverbial nail in the coffin of the progressive version of history.

The dynamic electoral process that existed under the Constitution's original design, tells us much of the challenges progressive politicians faced, as well as what institutional changes were needed to overcome them. Although a party majority in the State House and Senate would often guarantee a U.S. senator of that party, it did not guarantee agreement over a particular candidate, because the majority party often was a coalition of several factions supporting different U.S. Senate candidates. Progressives were among the ranks of these factions, which crossed party lines, but party platforms were not as rigid as they are today. This ensured Senate elections were hotly contested as much within parties as between them. Majority parties, because of the disagreements over specific issues, frequently disagreed on whom to nominate for a Senate seat. The challenge for the Progressive Movement, was that while the North and South effectively balanced each other ideologically, they needed the West to tip the scales. Although the movement was strong in the region, western progressives simply could not obtain a senior delegation. In Washington, influence is relative to seniority. The Senate, as an institution, provides senior members with chairmanships, preference on committee appointments, and other positions from which legislation is either pushed or tabled. The adoption of the 17th Amendment allowed them to overcome this obstacle.

Prior to the amendment, the differences between the average Senate tenure in western states and non-western states are significant. In fact, from 1870 – 1913, the average Senate tenure in the West was either constant, or in certain periods, was actually on the decline.[50] This disparity was bad news for progressive special

---

[48] Zywicki, Todd J. *Senators and Special Interests: A Public Choice Analysis of the Seventeenth Amendment.* pg. 1029 *Oregon Law Review* Vol. 73, University of Oregon School of Law, 1994
[49] Reference to a group of lawsuits challenging the constitutionality of economic regulation.
[50] Ibid. pg. 1052. By 1870, southern states had regained representation post-Civil War.

interest in the West, such as labor, as it put them at a significant disadvantage with the rest of the nation to secure federal funds. Following the passage of the amendment the trend is not only arrested, but also reversed, and the disparity disappears.[51] In addition to securing support for the Progressive Movement, rent-seeking special interest groups in western states were able to compete on equal footing in the bidding market that politicians have made out of our legislative process. In the lawmaking market, currency payments are in the form of political support for politicians, who then broker legislation by pairing supply and demand.[52] Increased Senate tenure protected wealth-producing legislation from reconsideration through *logrolling*, that is to say, a *quid pro quo*. Each legislator, in order to establish a majority coalition for their own legislation, pledges that they will support issues of importance to other members. Theoretically, if a member's tenure is uncertain, the chance of that member refusing to honor their pledge after their legislation is passed increases, thus decreasing a member's trustworthiness. In other words:

"In the extreme situation, if all legislators could serve only one term, all bills would have to be passed simultaneously or not at all. This would substantially raise the transaction costs [lobbying fees, bribes, and other perks] of passing legislation."[53]

The problem of "trustworthiness" – for both legislators and special interest – is easily alleviated through increased seniority. Senior legislators can be "trusted" to scratch each other's back, because they do not want to sabotage legislation they inevitably will sponsor in the future. If they want to ensure a majority coalition on subsequent bills, then their reputation must be that they can be "trusted" to follow the *quid pro quo*.

So, where do the American people fit into this treacherous plan to undermine our representative republican government? The answer is "rational ignorance."[54] Rational ignorance, in essence, is the product of structural distractions imposed upon the electorate by the powerful to remove the incentive, will, and ability among *We the People* to study the issues and vote accordingly. The term "low information voter," as understood by the American electorate, fails to capture the phenomena in its entirety. While stupidity implies a lack of intellectual capacity, ignorance implies ability when given adequate information. Through the rigors of meeting our economic necessities, misinformation campaigns and denying of

---

[51] Ibid. pg. 1053

[52] Tollison, Robert D. *Public Choice and Legislation*. pg. 343 *Virginia Law Review*. Vol. 74, No. 2 *Symposium on the Theory of Public Choice*. March, 1988

[53] Zywicki, Todd J. *Senators and Special Interests: A Public Choice Analysis of the Seventeenth Amendment*. pg. 1029 *Oregon Law Review* Vol. 73, University of Oregon School of Law, 1994

[54] Mueller, Dennis C. *Public Choice II: A Revised Edition*. pg. 205 – 206 Cambridge, MA: Cambridge University Press, 1989

education in absolute truth, the American people are intentional distracted away from using their God-given intellectual abilities. Those who live in the real world understand we exhaust our efforts to barely meet our basic hierarchy of heeds, or survive the daily grind. Much less time is available to follow the complexities of American politics. Through structural economic restraints and misinformation, or rather disinformation, special interest centralizes power by transferring wealth from a dispersed public to themselves.[55] Receptiveness to a populous message is born out of economic disparity, which ironically enough has been manufactured by the very same politicians who push the message.

Rent-seeking behavior from financial institutions, metal industries and labor unions, served not only to create the economic environment that led to the market failures of the 19th and 20th centuries, but the political support for pension reforms and other progressive programs that blunt our civil society. Wrestling the power away from our once-sovereign states was necessary to avoid the possibility of state legislatures sending those to Congress who would oppose wealth-producing legislation for special interest. The 17th Amendment was an effort to ensure the election of candidates who advocated for protectionist tariffs, labor contracts, and unconstitutional income taxes, which were needed to fund corrupt pension schemes, i.e. the GAR scheme. The adoption of the amendment demonstrated that special interest can manipulate the Constitution in the same manner they manipulate the legislative process.[56] Instead of being celebrated, the 17th Amendment should cause Americans to mourn the death of the Constitution's ability to restrain despotism. Absent the exercise of our constitutional obligation, which requires *We the People* to cast off rational ignorance, the Constitution is as much restrained by despotism as we have convinced ourselves despotism is restrained by the Constitution – if not more.

The fundamental alteration to our social contract strikes at the very heart of our founding principles, and the structure of American society. Our Constitution constructed a federal government of limited and enumerated powers. The loss of state sovereignty not only resulted in the destruction of our federalist system and the separation of powers, but the ability of the federal government at the behest of special interest to increase disparity by decreasing economic opportunity to the individual citizen. As politically unorganized and unaware individuals, we now have little recourse against this state of "democratic despotism," or otherwise democratic tyranny. Wealth and power, which at one time in America's history was dispersed around the country among *We the People*, is now hoarded and concentrated by special interest factions and their political allies.

As of 2012, 5 out of 10 of the wealthiest counties in America are in and

---

[55] Olson, Mancur. *The Logic of Collective Action: Public Goods and the Theory of Groups.* pg. 53 – 57 Cambridge, MA: Harvard University Press, 1965

[56] Zywicki, Todd J. *Senators and Special Interests: A Public Choice Analysis of the Seventeenth Amendment.* pg. 1055 *Oregon Law Review* Vol. 73, University of Oregon School of Law, 1994

around Washington D.C. and the surrounding suburbs, even though the area is home to only 5 percent of our nation's population.[57] Among the remaining 5 counties is Los Alamos, New Mexico. With a median annual household income of $103, 643, Los Alamo is the wealthiest county in the West United States. However, the county can credit the vast majority of their economic wealth to federal spending, as the largest employer is the Department of Energy's Los Alamos National Laboratory.[58] While 3 of the counties are suburbs in New Jersey that house Wall Street professionals willing to pay the state's high tax burden, they are unwilling to pay the even higher tax burden in the neighboring state of New York. Regardless, it represents the concentration of wealth and power among those in our society who are frequently the center of corruption and market failure at the expense of the less wealthy – Wall Street. It is true that wealthy Jersey suburbs, such as Hunterdon County, for the most part do not boast large amounts of government funding. But they are the recipients of wealth-producing legislation, or rents, which offer unfair competitive advantages to their industry. The second and only other western county among the wealthiest 10, Douglas County in Colorado, can contribute its wealth to economic freedom and 71 square miles of permanently protected land ineligible for imminent domain.[59] The early Douglas County Economic Development program promotes prosperity by attracting new business through a business-friendly regulatory and tax environment. Unfortunately, Agenda 21 now has a firm foothold in Douglas County's future economic development, therefore, it is only a matter of time before legal battles ensue.[60]

The protection of *We the People* against the excesses of factions, or special interest, was addressed in the original design of our Constitution, thus the need to amend the document. James Madison had to contend with a good deal of disagreement when he undertook the task of convincing the delegates at the Constitutional Convention to adopt our Constitution. Hedging against democratic despotism, however, was not one of them. The Founding Fathers were wise enough to fear "pure Democracy" as an option for our new republic. Madison wrote:

"The interference to which we are brought, is, that the causes of faction cannot be removed; and that relief is only to be sought in the means of controlling its effects. If a faction consists of less than a majority, relief is supplied by the republican principle, which enables the majority to defeat its sinister views by regular vote:... From this view of the subject, it may be concluded, that a pure Democracy, by which I mean, a Society, consisting of a

---

[57] Vardi, Nathan. *America's Richest Counties*. Forbes Magazine April 24th, 2012 and Kotkin, Joel. *The Expanding Wealth Of Washington*. Forbes Magazine March 19th, 2012
[58] Ibid.
[59] Ibid.
[60] http://www.douglas.co.us/cpsd/

small number of citizens, who assemble and administer the Government in person, can admit of no cure for the mischiefs of faction. A common passion or interest will, in almost every case, be felt by a majority of the whole; a communication and concert results from the form of Government itself; and there is nothing to check the inducements to sacrifice the weaker party, or of an obnoxious individual. Hence it is, that such Democracies have ever been spectacles of turbulence and contention; have ever been found incompatible with personal security, or rights of property; and have in general been as short in their lives, as they have been violent in their deaths. Theoretic politicians, who have patronized this species of Government, have erroneously supposed, that by reducing mankind to a perfect equality in their political rights, they would, at the same time, be perfectly equalized and assimilated in their possessions, their opinions, and their passions. A Republic, by which I mean a Government in which the scheme of representation takes place, opens a different perspective, and promises the cure for which we are seeking."[61]

Madison is making several observations, all of which are relevant to our discussion in this section. As did Adam Smith, Madison makes the very realistic observation that special interest is a political reality, whether we like it not. Government designed to protect *We the People* must be effective at limiting such elitist power. Democracy is ineffective, impractical, and dishonest to the ideals it professes. While politicians portray an ability of government to affect equality, order gives way to "infinite diversity or particular interests [and] dissonant opinions"; and the result is chaos.[62] Reason is lost to the passions of emotion, equality is redefined at the expense to individuality, and it is all done in vain as the despotic minority of the strong will inevitably "sacrifice" the weaker of society to meet their ends. In an act of what could only be defined as hubris, our political leaders have convinced us that they are capable of defying history, human nature, and the wisdom of our Founding Fathers.

As the 17th Amendment changed the relationship between the government and the individual citizen, it had profound psychological effects on the relationship between individual citizens. The Social Security Act of 1935, in fact, did just that by becoming the first example of a financial transaction directly from the federal government to the individual; and as we will examine in the following section, the act was essential to the progressive effort to manipulate the labor force. Aside from such spending being unsustainable, the growth of these programs continues to undermine the motivation of both the individual citizen and their community, to repair the family composition. What incentive do we have to care for our elderly family members, which strengthens the stability of the family unit, if the government promotes citizens to abort our societal

---

[61] Madison, James. *The Federalist* No. 10. *The Federalist Papers.* pg. 54 – 56 Edited by Garry Wills. New York: Banthan Dell, 2003

[62] John Randolph quoted in Bailyn, Bernard. *The Ideological Origins of the American Revolution.* pg. 284 Cambridge, MA: Belknap of Harvard University Press, 1992

obligations? In the past, America was renowned for our virtue in civil society and the strength of our families. Despite the efforts of the Progressive Movement to relieve citizens of our societal obligation, which the State has never been granted authority to do through Natural Law, somewhere the people's psychology drifted away from our founding principles. Locke, a dominant force in early American philosophy, wrote of our natural obligation applicable to old-age insurance:

"As He (God) hath laid on them an obligation to nourish, preserve, and bring up their offspring, so He has laid on the children a perpetual obligation of honoring their parents, which, containing in it an inward esteem and reverence to be shown by all outward expressions, ties up the child from anything that may ever injure or affront, disturb or endanger the happiness or life of those from whom he received his [life], and engages him in all actions of defense, relief, assistance, and comfort of those by whose means he entered into being and has been made capable of any enjoyments of life. From this obligation no state, no freedom, can absolve children."[63]

As we will examine further in chapter 3, the decay of the American family has taken a great toll on our society. Strong family composition provides individuals with the capacity to fulfill their own hierarchy of needs to the betterment of all in our society. Yet, we continue to weaken the pillars of power among the people, while funneling wealth and power to the government, who in turn, divides it among special interest. In fact, progressives have become so powerful that they have been able to rewrite history through our morally corrupt academic institutions. However, there has been a group who has benefited significantly from this transfer of power and wealth. In the following section, we will examine the evolution of unions, the role labor played in amending the Constitution, and their relationship to the state in the context of the prior section.

THE INVENTION OF RETIREMENT & THE MANUFACTURED CRISIS

Unions have become a source of immense controversy in modern American politics. They have experienced record membership declines, and as a result, have begun to fear their own waning political influence. Suffering a series of defeats at the hands of the *right to work* movement, for example in the once-impenetrable union state of Michigan, has caused unions to return to the use of violence.[64] Naturally, this has always been their preferred method of influence,

---

[63] Locke, John. *Second Essay Concerning Civil Government.* Great Books of the Western World, Vol. 35 pg. 39 Chicago: Encyclopedia Britannica, Inc. 1952
[64] Reference to government regulation of the contractual agreements between employers and labor unions that prevents them from excluding non-union workers, govern the extent to which an

but the umbrella of the progressive narrative has been successfully able to provide them shelter from public scrutiny. Furthermore, they have come to enjoy enormous political power, which up until now, made violence an unnecessary risk to their public perception. Labor unions, however, arose from the terrible working conditions created during the Gilded Age. Unfortunately, the proud historical character of common men exercising their rights of protection in order to demand that the artificial aristocracy respect their personhood, has been badly diminished and discredited within modern context. While they originally were purposed to check the power of the wealthy, they sought government influence to obtain the means to this end. Such is the nature of special interest; progressive politicians became beholden to union leaders for continued political support. Union leadership, unsurprisingly, have now become members of the very artificial aristocracy that they had once admirably opposed. Today, the voters alone remain as the sole check on union power, as there is no clear structural check on such entities within the amended Constitution. In the prior section, we discussed how the 17th Amendment enabled special interest to increase influence through rent-seeking, as well as ensure political support for the progressive agenda, such as public pensions. This section will discover what actions labor took to create the conditions necessary to push progressive reforms.

The rise of big labor was interdependent with the establishment of federal direct payments, or old-age insurance, in American political history. Both movements share in the fact that one could certainly argue industrialization as the reason for there existence, being the crisis of providing for superannuated workers, and other perceived ill treatments of labor. As Isaac Rubinow and Abraham Epstein were sounding the alarm on the need for pension reform, nefarious plots to manufacture crisis had already been in place. Labor had enormous culpability in the negative narrative being pushed against elderly workers. Although employers paid higher wages to senior workers, many found the amount of money to be a fair trade off for the social stability their businesses enjoyed.[65] Elderly workers exemplified the American mainstream Protestant work ethic, thus they were much more reliable than younger workers. Labor, on the other hand, despised older workers for their resistance to this new concept of retirement, and targeted younger workers for their willingness to cause disruption. While labor sought out younger workers to amass sufficient numbers to increase political influence, as far as older workers were concerned, employment was enough to be content. Working provided a higher standard of living than pensions and was dignifying, because it satisfied their duty to labor. A general acceptance among historians, although you would never know from

---

established union can require employees' membership, payment of dues, or fee as condition of employment. Prohibits union security agreements.

[65] Zieger, R.H. *The Development of Federal Old – Age Policy in the Era of the Great Depression: Pensions, Policies, and Politics 1920 – 1940.* Journal of Aging, Humanities, and the Arts pg. 253 July 1st 2008

modern political debate on labor issues, is that the culture of white older workers made labor interests difficult to achieve. William Graebner, wrote of the choice between these differences in attitude, which "For employers, this meant that older workers would be more likely to resist 'outside influences and agitation'."[66] What acknowledgement has not been made by historians, politicians and the like, is that the same political actors who advocated in favor of progressive reforms were creating the crisis of superannuated workers through the forced retirement of white elderly workers.

The alliance between progressives in government and labor had resolved to move elderly workers out of the workforce. In 1880, the labor participation rate for men age 65 and older stood at 78 percent, which represented a 2 percent increase from the prior three decades.[67] Industrialization, alone, could not have caused the crisis of superannuated workers, because the data trend shows a participation rate that was actually increasing in the 20 years following the Civil War. Furthermore, the decline in agriculture as an explanation is over-estimated. Labor force participation among black Americans was consistently higher than white older men. In 1900, some 90 percent of all black American households were in the agrarian South.[68] Excluding the period from 1900 – 1910, when farm values increased substantially, labor participation rates among older farmers from 1880 – 1940 was, on average, 9.3 percent higher than non-farmers.[69] The gap, therefore, between white and black participation rates cannot be explained regionally. Regardless of region, traditional explanations may have accounted for the decline to some degree, but an unnatural market force seemed to discriminately follow white older workers. Another popular progressive explanation, the old-age insurance provision of the Social Security Act of 1935, is equally insufficient. By 1930, prior to the laws implementation, the participation rate had already fallen to 58 percent.[70] In other words, more than half of the total decline occurred prior to 1942, when the first payments were made. Prior to the Depression, there is an apparent downward trend in older working whites, which runs counter to the trend of black Americans, and indeed, the workforce as a whole.[71]

During the period from the 1880s – 1930s, labor successfully lobbied for mandatory retirement legislation in labor prone industries. Older age workers

---

[66] Graebner, W. *A History of Retirement: The meaning and function of an American institution, 1885 – 1978.* pg. 39 Connecticut: Yale University Press, 1980

[67] Source: U.S. Census Bureau, see Costa, Dora L. *The Evolution of Retirement: An American Economic History, 1880-1990.* Chicago: University of Chicago Press, 1998.

[68] Maloney, Thomas N. *African Americans in the Twentieth Century.* EH.Net Encyclopedia, Edited by Robert Whaples, January 18th, 2002

[69] Lee, Chulhee. *Sectoral Shift and the Labor-Force Participation of Older Males in the United States, 1880-1940.* pg. 512 – 523 *Journal of Economic History* 62, no. 2, 2002

[70] Figure 2.2: Progressive Era Labor Participation Rate

[71] Ibid.

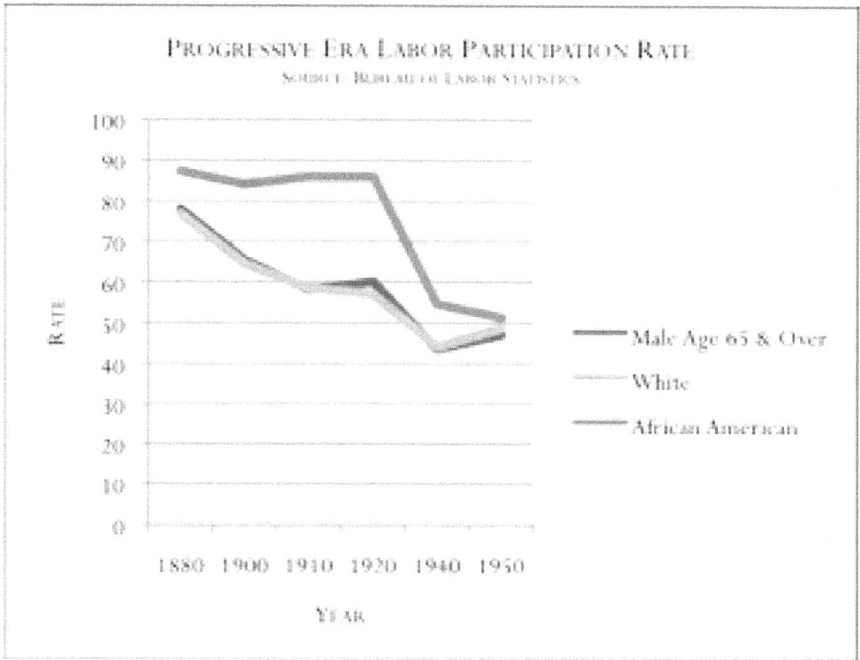

Figure 2.2: Whereas the labor participation among men 65 and over was once the vast majority, a significant disparity between white and black Americans reflected how industry targeted white male workers 65 years and over. Consequently, black Americans have been enticed away from their work ethic, as the entire rate for all ages today is only 61.3 percent.

certainly resisted labor's efforts, but industry cost-cutting concerns, labor agitations, federal legislation, and so on, began to force them out. In the case of Detroit and the automobile industry, older workers were not exactly begging for an old-age pension. In reality, quite the contrary was true. Embedded within the work habits of the American labor force was the idea of their duty of calling to labor, and indeed, they wanted to work:

"During the springtime rehiring season in Detroit, stores stocked extra supplies of black shoe polish, which older workers daubed on their hair to disguise tell-tale patches of gray."[72]

It is certainly worth mentioning that the progressive agenda throughout the 20th century advanced toward the same goal, and as of April of 2013, the labor force participation rate for all adults age 65 and over, was only 6.9 percent.[73] The goal of the Progressive Movement has been to remove the autonomous and

---

[72] Zieger, R.H. *The Development of Federal Old – Age Policy in the Era of the Great Depression: Pensions, Policies, and Politics 1920 – 1940.* Journal of Aging, Humanities, and the Arts pg. 254 July 1st 2008
[73] April BLS employment report: http://www.bls.gov/news.release/pdf/empsit.pdf

empowering American identity, which has long been the happiness-producing trait that results from the Protestant ethic. A strong federal government did not serve as a savior to either of these reforms, which is the claim by the progressive narrative, but rather these issues were exploited as a part of the enduring quest to concentrate power to the federal government. However, in order to understand the deception used to meet these ends we have to examine the historical role that labor played as an interest group during the Progressive Era. Progressives had learned a valuable lesson from the setbacks they had realized at the end of the 19th century. Nebraska Senator Norris Brown, was equally as forward-thinking as his state's congressman, William Jennings Bryan. He saw the highest court in the land as an obstacle to obtaining permanent federal authority to implement the progressive agenda. Specifically regarding the issue of federal taxation, which was necessary to fund public projects and pension reform, he argued progressives needed to pass and ratify such an amendment "which will give the court a Constitution that cannot be interpreted two ways."[74]

The passage of the 17th Amendment was part of a logrolling deal with the 16th Amendment, which affirmed the constitutionality of unapportioned progressive federal income tax. In *Pollock v. Farmers' Loan & Trust Co.* (1895), the Supreme Court ruled that the Income Tax Act of 1894 was, in essence, a series of direct taxes that violated various sections of Article I in the Constitution. Although the 16th Amendment was proposed first, ratification was held up by the North until interventionist politicians with alliances to business could be assured the new revenues would not go to the South.[75] Progressive politicians understood that until the 17th Amendment was ratified, a new proposed federal income tax burden would disproportionately affect the northern states. The 17th Amendment would ensure, especially in the long-term, that the western states could increase their seniority in the Senate, thus special interest influence that directed the new federal revenues. In the short-term, in exchange for supporting the 16th Amendment the North demanded a greater share of the federal budget.[76] Western support for the 17th Amendment was significant relative to the other regions. The Populist Party's brief earlier presence, coupled with progressives in both major parties, dominated the political narrative of economic disparity in the West. Among the interest groups that stood to benefit the most from the passage of the 17th Amendment, and had a capable cross-regional presence, were the labor unions.

The passage of a constitutional amendment to reform senatorial elections,

---

[74] Ekirch, Arthur A. Jr. *The Sixteenth Amendment: The Historical Background.* Vol. 1, No. 1 pg. 173 *Cato Journal,* Washington, DC: Spring, 1981
[75] Grimes, Alan Pendleton. *Democracy and the Amendments to the Constitution.* pg. 66 – 74 Lexington, MA: Lexington, 1978
[76] Baack, Bennett D., and Edward John Ray. *Special Interests and the Adoption of the Income Tax in the United States. The Journal of Economic History* 45.03, 1985: 607.

therefore, was contingent upon Congress climbing the steep hill of income tax imposition. For decades, labor had been knee deep in efforts to ensure substantial revenues were available to fund profitable public projects. In the 1870s, politicians in both parties had found an alliance on the issue of taxation in the Greenback Labor Party.[77] The issue remained a third rail to mainstream elements within the two major parties, although by the 1890s progressive taxation appeared in the platforms of both the People's Party and the Socialist Labor Party. During the election of 1892, the issue of taxation seemed to have taken a back seat to more pressing issues, such as *Free Silver*, tariffs, and corruption. Policies implemented under President Harrison had begun to take a grave toll on the American economy. Two pieces of progressive legislation created market conditions ripe for economic crisis.

Tariffs on imports had already been substantial before Congress passed the Tariff Act of 1890, otherwise known as the McKinley Tariff. The arguments in favor of high tariffs varied. Protectionists supposedly favored government intervention in the market to give American businesses a competitive advantage. Following the Civil War, many politicians claimed that elevated tariffs would serve to pay off debt incurred during the war. By the early 1880s, however, the federal government was already running a large surplus. As this revelation became more susceptible to public scrutiny the argument shifted in favor of even higher tariffs to decrease the surplus. The logic was based on a twisted interpretation of what we now identify as the *Laffer Curve*.[78] Modern economists and economic historians continue to perpetuate this inappropriate analogy. In 19th century America, there were little to no domestic markets for certain goods, such as carpet wool, raw sugar and tin plates, thus they needed to be imported despite the tariff increase. Modern American markets have much more robust competition, therefore, avoidance behavior transpires. Nevertheless, stacked with some 450 amendments, the passage of the McKinley Tariff increased average tariff duties from 38 percent to 49.5 percent.[79] Pro-business conservatives, referred to as the "Bourbons," opposed tariffs and subsidies in favor of classical liberalism, or laissez-faire.[80] They believed it immoral for progressives to reward the special interests of big business and labor with tariffs that would increase the cost of goods. Indeed, the McKinley Tariff placed a heavy burden on American consumers without achieving any of the progressives' stated goals. The only realized decrease in revenues was a meager 4 percent, and that

---

[77] Ratner, Sidney. *Taxation and Democracy in America*. Chp. 8 New York: Wiley, 1967
[78] Reference to Reaganomics advisor Art Laffer, who argued that higher tax burdens lead to less revenue. However, theory was in respect to domestic taxes in 1980, not tariffs in 1880.
[79] Reitano, Joanne. *The Tariff Question in the Gilded Age: The Great Debate of 1888*. pg. 129 University Park, PA: Pennsylvania State University Press, 1994
[80] Reference to wing of Democratic party; conservative pro-business but no tariff protections, believed in strict competition w/o government intervention.

was due to the exemption of raw sugar; of which, at the time brought in more revenue than any other import on the tariff duty list.[81] The price of goods spiked as progressive special interest in labor and metal works enjoyed the spoils. Meanwhile, individual consumers and American farmers were suffering the economic disparity produced by crony capitalism.

The debts incurred by American farmers became harder to repay, as consumer demand was sapped from the economy. Farmers found themselves overproducing and sending to market a supply of goods that had little value. Proponents of *Free Silver*, known as "Silverites," argued that the coinage of silver would cause inflation, making it easier for farmers to pay off their debts. In fact, everybody was in agreement with the prospect of cheap money causing inflation. Conservative Bourbons argued against the dangers of inflation, preferring either the reduction or elimination of protectionist supported tariffs, which would seem to have been the logical policy. Of course, logic had nothing to do with the Silverites' position. Miners complained that the cost of extracting silver, which they had a substantial supply of on hand already, was proving the metal unprofitable to mine. Lobbied by the mining industry, including mining labor, progressive politicians were more concerned with the oversupply of silver than agrarian goods. Nevertheless, the economic hardship experienced by the farmers gravitated them toward the populist progressive message, because it was falsely sold as a win-win solution. They allied with elements of the soon to be former Greenback Labor Party, and would later be known as the People's Party, or the Populists. Enacted in conjunction with the Tariff Act of 1890, the Silver Purchase Act required the federal government to purchase 4.5 million ounces of silver every month.[82] The artificially inflated demand for silver had the effect on price the miners were hoping it would, but with unintended consequences.

Contrary to progressive economic theory, the nature of a market economy is such that monetary policy does not occur in a vacuum. As the price of silver began to rise people still redeemed the cheaper notes for gold, not silver, depleting the government's gold reserves. As gold became dangerously low, silver could no longer be redeemed at current value. Although progressive historians often blame overbuilding in the railroad industry, loans, unforeseen events in the Argentinean financial markets, and even the repeal of the Silver Purchase Act itself, the Panic of 1893 had already been underway as a result of tariffs and misguided intervention in monetary policy.[83] Inflation ran rampant without the stabilizing power of gold. Ultimately, J.P. Morgan stepped in to loan the federal government a substantial amount of gold in order to build up federal

---

[81] Irwin, Douglas A. *Did Late-Nineteenth-Century U.S. Tariffs Promote Infant Industries? Evidence from the Tinplate Industry*. The Journal of Economic History Vol. 60, No. 2 (Jun., 2000), pp. 335-360
[82] Socolofsky, Homer and Spetter, Allen B. *The Presidency of Benjamin Harrison*. pg. 58 Lawrence: University of Kansas Press, 1987
[83] Ibid. pg. 59

reserves, thus avoiding a complete currency collapse.

The economic pain leading up to the Panic of 1893, led to former President Grover Cleveland's victory in the election of 1892. He had been president and served from 1885 – 1889, but as a result of progressive fraud, had been defeated by President Harrison while running for re-election.[84] President Cleveland had a long history of fighting corruption, government waste, tariffs, and because of this, labor and progressives hated him. As Mayor of Buffalo, he had vetoed a street sweeping contract when he discovered the highest bidder was awarded the project due to his political connections. This put him on the receiving end of attacks from the infamous Tammany Hall machine, which haunted him through his New York gubernatorial bid, and later his nomination for president. President Cleveland wrote in his response, "I regard it as the culmination of a most bare-faced, impudent, and shameless scheme to betray the interests of the people, and to worse than squander the public money".[85] In his first term, he opposed Free Silver, tariffs and protectionism, vetoed hundreds of corrupt pension scheme bills, and pushed for the passage of the Dawes Act. The proposal appropriated land within Indian territories to individual tribal members in the hope that it would lift them out of poverty through empowerment. Unfortunately, as we will discuss in the following chapter, predictably the federal government failed to live up to their agreement. With President Cleveland, and the Bourbon wing of his party out of the way, progressives implemented the two major policies the Bourbons had opposed.

In the beginning of his second term the economic depression hit the American economy. The repeal of the Silver Purchase Act was priority number one, and in fact, passed with overwhelming support. Markets quickly reacted favorably, as proponents of gold knew it would, and Treasury reserve levels returned to stabilizing levels.[86] The tension between the Cleveland administration and labor, however, was made worse with the repeal of the Silver Purchase Act. Jacob S. Coxey, a progressive politician from Ohio, led a labor march to Washington D.C. to protest the administration. Beginning in Massillon Ohio, the group of "workingmen" agitated society everywhere they passed through, demanding public funds be appropriated for national road projects.[87] Their numbers dwindled before they even made it across the Ohio River, and of those who did, many were arrested for trespassing on the Capitol Hill lawn. To be fair, it was a time of great economic hardship. However, the legislation that labor lobbied Congress to pass was, in large part, responsible for the economic destabilization. The importance of the strike was that it served as a warning for how far labor

---

[84] Jeffers, H. Paul. *An Honest President: The Life and Presidencies of Grover Cleveland.* pg. 220 – 222 New York: W. Morrow, 2000

[85] Nevins, Allan. *Grover Cleveland; a Study in Courage.* pg. 85 New York: Dodd, Mead & Co., 1932

[86] Graff, Henry F. *Grover Cleveland.* pg. 115 New York: Times, 2002

[87] Ibid. pg. 117 – 118

would be willing to go to get legislation passed that favored labor, no matter the cost. As is always the case with collectivism, the well-being of the whole of society only survives in rhetoric. Democratic tyranny will always put the needs of the few and the strong above the weak and unrepresented.

Eugene V. Debs, leader of the American Railway Union and future five time Socialist Party presidential candidate, organized what would be known as the Pullman Strike. Named after the Pullman Company, where the strike originally began, the movement ballooned to over 125,000 activists nationwide, bringing much of the nation's commerce to a grinding halt. But private industry wasn't President's Cleveland's rationale for intervening. The railways carried the nation's mail and many of them were currently in federal bankruptcy as a result of the economic depression.[88] Although President Cleveland received bipartisan praise, and even had a consensus within partisan publications, labor used the crisis to mobilize workers just in time for the congressional elections of 1894.[89] It was widely viewed that President Cleveland and the Bourbons could not complete the economic turnaround, because his history with labor was partly the cause of the widespread strikes. However, never was labor held accountable for exacerbating the economy with strikes and demonstrations. The progressive factions, drawing support away from Populist and Socialist Labor Parties, united under the Republican Party and regained control of the House of Representatives. Even within Cleveland's own Democratic Party, the progressive wing – led by Williams Jennings Bryan – seized control of the majority down the ballot.

The progressive majority would again move on their commitment to pass an income tax, which would ultimately fail to live up to constitutional scrutiny. The Wilson-Gorman tariff bill did not reduce tariffs significantly, however, it contained the income tax provision of 1894. For all of the progressive arguments making the case for popularly elected senators, it was in the Senate and in the hands of progressive special interest where the bill went awry. Initially, the 2 percent income tax was supposed to make up for the loss of revenue due to the reduction in tariffs. That may have been true had the bill lowered tariffs significantly, as did the version introduced and passed through the House of Representatives. Congressman Wilson of West Virginia, supported by President Cleveland, reduced the tariff to zero on iron ore, wool, lumber and coal. There was considerable opposition in the House from protectionist progressives, but William Jennings Bryan along with his Populist Party support was able to build a strong enough coalition to pass the measure.[90] Maryland Senator Arthur P.

---

[88] Jeffers, H. Paul. *An Honest President: The Life and Presidencies of Grover Cleveland*. pg. 296 – 297 New York: W. Morrow, 2000

[89] Ibid. pg. 304 – 305

[90] Ekirch, Arthur A. Jr. *The Sixteenth Amendment: The Historical Background.* Vol. 1, No. 1 pg. 167 *Cato Journal,* Washington, DC: Spring, 1981

Gorman, acting as the go-to guy for the protectionist lobby, attached more than 600 special interest amendments that nullified reform measures and again raised tariff rates. President Cleveland, who had promised tariff reform, thought the measure was the lesser of the two evils. The tariff rates were not at the levels proposed by Wilson, but the McKinley Tariff Act was even more severe. Although he regarded the new legislation as corrupt, he had little choice but to allow the bill to go into law without his signature.

The real history of labor teaches us several lessons, which taken in concert with the entire Progressive Movement raises our awareness to the consequences that arise from relying on government-centered solutions. Progressivism is an ideology and not a political party. Aside from the historical value to our cost-benefit analysis, the 1880s exemplify the obfuscation that can arise when we assign a political party one particular ideology. The confusion only increases when we examine party platforms in the early 20th century. The ability of the Progressive Movement to hold together constituencies, whose interests are obviously in conflict, arises from a rational ignorance to the ideology itself. Agrarian aspirations to lower tariffs were in conflict with labor's interest, nevertheless, the Greenback Labor Party evolved to include farmers. The coalition became known as the Populists and ensured the passage of the Wilson-Gorman tariff bill, which contained the progressive income tax. The same is true regarding the policy of Free Silver. The antimonopoly populist message resonated across politically organized groups who would have otherwise viewed themselves as wholly incompatible. Rhetoric and rational ignorance clouded the economic realities of Free Silver, which mining labor desperately supported, but clearly did not benefit American farmers – despite them being led to believe that it would.

This dynamic can be seen throughout the labor movement in the 20th century. Although progressives claim the mantle of civil rights activism, the original Wagner Act, which established the National Labor Relations Board provided collective bargaining rights to labor, while intentionally excluding black Americans. The OAI provision in the Social Security Act of 1935 was intentionally aimed at industrial labor, which was overwhelmingly white and male.[91] The exclusion of black Americans from old-age pension benefits was directly due to the union lobby's demands. In modern America, the stranglehold that teacher unions have on public education relegates minorities to poverty stricken neighborhoods with failed school systems. Meanwhile, wealthy progressives send their children to the school of their choice. Newark Teachers Union leader Joseph Del Grosso, attended private school as a child, yet he refuses to empower minority parents with the same choice his mother had. Black Americans understand their children are subjected to downtrodden schools, which prevents future upward mobility, but they continue to support

---

[91] Zieger, R.H. *The Development of Federal Old – Age Policy in the Era of the Great Depression: Pensions, Policies, and Politics 1920 – 1940.* Journal of Aging, Humanities, and the Arts pg. 263 July 1st 2008

progressives. This is no longer the case in New Orleans, however, where school choice post-Katrina has given black Americans opportunities that did not exist before Katrina destroyed the public school system. Reason needs real world results in order to effectively combat the populist message, such as the case now in Louisiana. Education will be discussed in more detail in the following chapter, but it demonstrates this incredible political phenomena. That is to say, the progressive ability to convince people with zero-sum interests that government can meet all their demands in a win-win result. The meaning and role for "Big Brother" has been twisted to promote a delusion that we can play a zero-sum game without someone losing. Americans must lose this illusion. Class warfare, social agitations, fear speech and rational ignorance, all have made emotionally charged straw man arguments powerful political weapons against reason and truth.

But rhetoric alone cannot explain the success of the Progressive Movement. In truth, American progressives were familiar with the methods used in Europe to increase the size and scope of government – all the better to profess in the name of social justice.[92] In true progressive fashion, the 16th Amendment was sold to the public as an effort to tax the wealthy, and of course, only if it's "necessary and proper" to do so or, in a so-called emergency. On the floor of the House of Representatives, New York Congressman Sereno Payne claimed that, although he was "utterly opposed to it," we may find it necessary in the future:

"I deem it essential to the future existence of the nation, should we have a great war, which God forbid, that we have the power to exhaust every resource of taxing our people to carry on the war with vigor, with the prestige that has hitherto come to the American people, and that we should not have the national hand paralyzed because of its inability under the Constitution of the United States to reach its hand out and gather these taxes and all others from the citizens of the United States, whose Government we are protecting."[93]

The result, however, was an expedited tax and a code that would soon be carved out to benefit the wealthy, while the burden disproportionately fell on middle class Americans. In 1914, revenues were a disappointing $28 million dollars, however, the upward trend was clear. For dissenters, well, we can always whip up a war, or another crisis. It wouldn't be long for Congressman Sereno's comments to be proven prophetical, as the wartime collections began to climb into the billions. As for the tax falling on wealthy citizens, from 1940 – 1945, the number of personal returns filed increased from less than fifteen million to just under fifty million citizens. What started as a supposed tax on class, "became a

---

[92] Ekirch, Arthur A. Jr. *The Sixteenth Amendment: The Historical Background.* Vol. 1, No. 1 pg. 172 *Cato Journal,* Washington, DC: Spring, 1981
[93] Ibid. pg. 174

mass, rather than a class, levy."[94] Previous attempts to implement progressive taxes during and after the Civil War, which Mark Twain scoffed at, had resulted in the same avoidance behavior seen on tariff duties. Whether on raw goods or manufactured, tariffs certainly hurt Americans with lower income more than the profits of the wealthy. The sentiment did grow strong to lower tariffs, which enabled progressives to finally implement an unpopular income tax; but of course, it was an emergency. If rhetoric was sufficient, then we should not see periodic swings in the electorate when the results of progressive policies are exposed in everyday American life. The manufacture and exploitation of crisis has served to fill this void.

Fear is the basis for the progressive ideology, and the most frequently exploited emotion in American politics. Fear of individuals, families and communities, who may not meet their hierarchy of needs runs deep in the human psyche. It is natural to react to the perceived causes of our fellow citizens' suffering. Our susceptibility to progressivism actually speaks to the goodness of humankind. Since this apparently seems to be true of human behavior, well then I submit Abraham Maslow is right, and Freud is wrong. Inherently, human beings are good, merely capable of nefarious behavior when morally bankrupt. Perceiving labor conditions, which were atrocious and unaccountable, as a cause of suffering naturally led to the desire to pull together in what resembles a community – a union. It isn't natural, however, when those perceptions are inaccurate and manufactured for political gain. Progressives, including labor, manufacture crisis through agitations, social and economic interventions, while serving the needs of special interests at the expense of societal happiness. As they did during the Civil War, the Panic of 1893, both World Wars, the Great Depression, and most recent the Great Recession, they exploit our fears and assure measures which will certainly restrict our freedoms are temporary. During the Civil War, the tax was proposed as a temporary measure, yet even when the government was running a surplus they refused to give up federal payments they were directing to special interest. They blamed the overbuilding of railways for the Panic of 1893, yet the American Railway Union pushed for their construction. Had the Silver Purchase Act of 1890 not been passed at the behest of mining interests, then federal gold reserves would have never depleted. In 1894, at the height of the depression, they used fear and class warfare to pass unpopular income tax legislation. Predictably, the tariffs were not even lowered to the levels that would have required the federal government to collect an income tax.[95]

In politics, the biggest enemy of reason is fear, and it stems from our desire to meet our human needs. If articulated powerfully, rational ignorance can be overwhelmed by the reason of Natural Law. Government politicians, even if they

[94] Ibid. pg. 182
[95] Ibid.

truly intended, cannot be everything to everyone. In times of crisis, however, ideology is amplified by fear, and reason is almost unrealizable. Surprisingly, the idea that the politically ambitious would manufacture crisis to meet their own ends is often met with extreme skepticism – even mockery. But for those who understand Natural Law this is the only possible outcome. What is more concerning is that progressives found so many areas of society to exploit, and that these despots have been enormously successful in doing so. Barbara C. Clark, whom I referenced in the beginning of the chapter is wrong in her analysis. Americans didn't "face the limits of human virtue," we abandoned human virtue, because there are no "limits" to human potential in a virtuous republic and the pre-Progressive Era history demonstrated as much. Bombarded by incessant crisis, we have allowed the politicians to convince us that government could supplement civil society and care for our hierarchy of needs.[96] Naturally, the result has not been empowerment or the enjoyment of full citizenship by minorities, the middle class, the poor or the helpless. In the next section, we will discuss prior attempts to explain their success, periods of pushback by the American people, and why these past efforts to rollback government have failed.

THE REST IS HISTORY

In the seminal work of economist Robert Higgs, *Crisis and Leviathan*, he describes what is called "the ratchet effect."[97] In periods of American history when we measure pre-crisis and post-crisis levels in the size and scope of government, we can conclude two changes have occurred. First, post-crisis levels will reveal we have realized an increase in the size and scope of government from the pre-crisis level. Even in a studied duration of normal government growth, the means by which it grows can only be accounted for by the conditions of the last crisis. Second, the retrenchment that follows is never sufficient to return government to the pre-crisis level. We get into dangerous territory when we narrowly interpret government growth in traditional terms relative to GDP, or gross domestic product. Economic measurements such as government spending as a percentage of GDP, overlook far too many elements to the phenomena of government growth, which permits despotic movement right underneath our noses. He explains "the essence of Big Government" and government growth, in such a manner a raised awareness reveals almost endless encroachments on our constitutional social contract:

---

[96] Smith, Barbara Clark. *The Revolution Preserved Social Inequality.* The William and Mary Quarterly, 3rd Series Vol. L1, Number 4, pg. 2 Oct. 1994

[97] Higgs, Robert. *Crisis and Leviathan: Critical Episodes in the Growth of American Government.* New York: Oxford University Press, 1987

"I have argued that high levels of governmental taxing, spending, and employment derive from but are not themselves the essence of Big Government; the essence is a wide scope of effective authority over economic decision-making. Authority comes first: no authority, then no taxing, spending, or employment. Authority arises from executive orders, statutes, court decisions, and the directives of regulatory agencies."[98]

Disputing the tendency by economists, political scientists, and historians to use quantitative measures to chart the growth of government is best left to Mr. Higgs. I would certainly agree with his premise. Furthermore, I view these efforts at best, as intentional attempts to mislead, and at worst, extensions of the manufactured crisis itself; perhaps, even a preparatory conditioning for the next crisis to follow. Regardless, his findings of a ratchet effect are clear and should lead us to next discover the psychological and cultural reasons government growth has become so "necessary and proper." While I am focusing on the expansion of the federal government, or the centralization of power, I by no means wish to dismiss the growth of other levels, such as state, city and local/county governments. There can be no doubt that the reality of everyday American life, which is tantamount to one in a police state, is dictated in great measure by all levels of government. The question I now pose is a simple one: why do we tolerate living like this? Although the growth of government, which by any measurable method has been staggering in the last 100 plus years, by majority Americans have remained ideologically conservative. Conservative politicians, or professed conservatives at least, have disappointed constituents without any substantial roll back of government authority. Yet, they are allowed to carry on careerism meeting no considerable resistance. Despite the political pendulum swinging back to the conservative movement, in reality, the campaign rhetoric, has not produced significant reform to the domestic progressive agenda. For the most part, the federal government has retained the new authorities it had assumed after the World Wars, and in some cases, expanded them dramatically. Throughout the mid-late 20th century, there were three main opportunities to ride the ideological momentum and reduce the size and scope of government.

Following the New Deal, which historians break up into two separate periods, a coalition of conservatives from both parties made considerable gains in congressional elections. It was, however, still a time of war and economic suffering – or, a crisis – and a great number of citizens could not meet even the most basic of human needs. Little attention was being paid to the enormous structural changes in government under Roosevelt, which further expanded government into the economy, making possible the modern crony capitalist state in America today.[99] Even more significant, President Roosevelt was popular and

---

[98] Ibid. pg. 32
[99] Stockman, David A. *The Great Deformation: The Corruption of Capitalism in America.* Philadelphia, PA: Perseus Books Group, 2013

answered little for his assault on the Supreme Court after its partial repudiation of his socialist agenda. In 1961, President Kennedy said, "And so, my fellow Americans: ask not what your country can do for you – ask what you can do for your country," but just three years later, the Democratic landslide of 1964 led to the most liberal House of Representatives since 1938.[100] Opposition to Great Society reforms, such as the Social Security Act of 1965, didn't stand at chance. Democrats gained enough seats to control more than two-thirds of each chamber and President Johnson won roughly 61 percent of the popular vote, carrying all but six states. The crisis in Vietnam and the loss of a president to an assassin's rifle added to the psychology of crisis, which quickly faded along with Johnson's popularity. The "silent majority" gave Nixon a healthy electoral vote victory in 1968, and a landslide in 1972, but President Nixon was a foreign policy conservative and a domestic progressive. Nixon demolished the idea of fiscal discipline and dropped the gold-backed dollar, which has greatly contributed to the delusional mentality that debt is inconsequential.[101] Gerald Ford is wholly inconsequential, that is to say, he displayed and governed little by the principles of conservatism. The third and final conservative swing can be identified as the period beginning with President Reagan, and ending with President Clinton. To be sure, William Jefferson Clinton is a devout progressive. His January 27th radio address, in which he claimed that "the era of big government is over," was not written into the speech because that was President Clinton's desired outcome, but rather his only hope for political survival.[102] The transformative statement made by President Reagan during his inaugural speech almost 15 years earlier to the day, set political parameters for President Clinton. To be seen as mainstream, progressives had to keep the perception that they agreed with President Reagan when he said:

"In this present crisis, government is not the solution to our problem; government is the problem. From time to time we've been tempted to believe that society has become too complex to be managed by self-rule, that government by an elite group is superior to government for, by, and of the people. Well, if no one among us is capable of governing himself, then who among us has the capacity to govern someone else? All of us together, in and out of government, must bear the burden. The solutions we seek must be equitable, with no one group singled out to pay a higher price."[103]

Of course, in times of crisis progressives exploit our fears rather than calm them.

---

[100] References in pop culture to the most liberal Congress since 1938 were widespread and claimed as such in LIFE Magazine. Nov. 5th, 1965
[101] Stockman, David A. *The Great Deformation: The Corruption of Capitalism in America*. Philadelphia, PA: Perseus Books Group, 2013
[102] President William Jefferson Clinton's Radio Address to the Nation, January 27th 1996
[103] President Ronald Wilson Reagan's Inaugural Address to the Nation, January 20th, 1981

They share the Hamiltonian view that "the rich and well-born" should govern through their "permanent share of government," and place in the American psyche the possibility "that society has become too complex to be managed by self-rule."[104] The American political psychology in the latter part of the 20th century was personified in President Ronald Reagan, whose words of empowerment demonstrate he was a man of incredible virtue. Progressives remained relevant through entitlement programs, and by masquerading as the "light beer" version of Reagan conservatism. Conservatives failed to recapture the American political psychology entirely, however, as they neglected both the structural and cultural changes implemented during the Progressive Era.

As examined in the prior two sections, the adoption of both the 16th and 17th Amendments and federal judicial activists, have fundamentally changed the terms of our American social contract. Although originally sold to the public and falsely perpetuated to our children as a victory against nonexistent straw men, these amendments have granted an excess of powers to the despots in the federal government, which are incompatible with any future promise of liberty. Any successful attempt to roll back the damage done to our society, which is contingent upon restoring republicanism, must at some point address the structural defilements to our Constitution. The outright repeal of these amendments would be difficult to say the least - if not impossible. The prevailing economic theory of the constitutional amendment process predicts that, besides the difficulties in satisfying the requirements of Article V of the Constitution, politicians and special interest will do everything in their power to protect their investments and revenue streams.[105] While I have focused on the two major authority granting amendments, in fact, the vast majority of post-Bill of Rights amendments to the Constitution were found to increase agency cost, thus further increasing rent-seeking behavior and facilitating the expansion of the federal government.[106] Threatening the power source of the powerful will no doubt be met will vociferous opposition. There are two conservative ideas, which if each were to be passed in concert, would forcibly "starve the beast" and restrain its power, if only temporarily.

If Americans wish to disallow politicians to pit them against each other, then the federal government's tax policy must be reformed. Progressive income tax is more than an economic policy, for progressives, it is also a social policy as well. If all citizens are equal, then how can we reconcile such an inequitable policy? The presumption that the Tax Policy Center, Brookings, and other government go-to think-tanks who oppose any form of a flat tax are non-partisan organizations, is a fallacy. These institutions are, and long have been, mere extensions of the

---

[104] Ibid. Hamilton quote from section I.

[105] Boudreaux, Donald J. and Pritchard, A.C. *Rewriting the Constitution: An Economic Analysis of the Constitutional Amendment Process*. pg. 157 – 159 62 Fordham Law Review 111, 1993

[106] Ibid. pg. 140 – 152

government bureaucracy. Independent economic studies conducted by Paul Bachman, Jonathan Haughton, Laurence J. Kotlikoff, Alfonso Sanchez-Penalver, David G. Tuerck, and many others have concluded a flat tax could indeed remain revenue neutral.[107] For progressives, it seems perfectly acceptable to carve out loopholes to any and every special interest group with an office on K Street, but utterly ridiculous to impose a flat tax with only one loophole for lower income Americans. Reforming the progressive tax code has little to do with protecting the poor, and more to do with protecting the ability of politicians to offer special interest "factions" wealth-producing legislation. Studies of post-communist Russia's tax reform, such as the one conducted by Denvil R. Duncan of Indiana University, reveals a decrease in avoidance behavior and, both increases in revenues as well as compliance.[108] Perhaps of paramount concern to progressive politicians, as was the case in communist Russia, is that they will lose the ability to exploit class warfare animosity, thus divide and conquer. Aside from receiving a political payment for tax code loopholes, economic disparity is one of the powerful weapons progressives have in their arsenal, which they rely on to perpetuate "rational ignorance." As Americans struggle to survive the structural gauntlet politicians have manufactured to distract us, economic disparity ensures the efficiency of class warfare's ability to resonate in our psyches.

Propose to remove the federal government's power to tax, and assuredly a plurality of Americans would be ecstatic. Propose to remove their ability to take a popular vote on their elected senator, and they will be furious. I would express little optimism in the prospect that even the most-heavily funded messaging campaign would ever be able to succeed at such an undertaking. Likewise, nothing short of a sustainable conservative reawakening over a significant duration of time would be needed to strip government's excessive regulatory authority. High court decisions reversing previous rulings, such as *Munns v. Illinois* (1877), would require a considerable amount of time due to the life tenure of Supreme Court Justices. Naturally, even if such a court would be appointed, it would need the credibility of a constitutional amendment to add validity to their ruling. A solution that would certainly be more palatable, as well as address the underlying problem, would be the imposition of term limits. Term limits would satisfy purists who believe in the fairness of popular senatorial elections, as well as remove the corrupt *quid pro quo*. Uncertain tenure would make uncertain a members "trustworthiness," thereby reducing corruption that stems from seniority. If increased seniority was the original obstacle to rent-seeking, then clearly term limit imposition would effectively reduce the influence of special interest. For a change, members of Congress would be somewhat free

---

[107] Bachman, Haughton, Kotlikoff, Sanchez-Penalver, Tuerk. *Taxing Sales Under the Fair Tax: What Rate Works?* Beacon Hill Institute. *Tax Analysts.* Suffolk University, 2007

[108] Denvil, Duncan R. *Economic Impact of a "Flat" Tax. What Have We Learned From The Russian Experience.* School of Public and Environmental Affairs Insights. Indiana University, 2012

to vote according to their conscience.

While the previous propositions address structural government reformations, none of them have the potential to ensure the permanency of liberty. The original design of the Constitution, our federalist system of government, etc., provided far more structural restriction on potential abuses of power, which ultimately, the powerful were capable of manipulating. Limiting *We the People* to structural solutions alone is an exercise in futility, as those structures are sure to be subject to the "ratchets" of government growth. The answer can only be found in the original source of rational ignorance. That is to say, abandoning principled education in Natural Law resulted in citizens defaulting on our civic obligations, which over time gave those in government an excuse to exercise new "necessary and proper" authorities. America slowly underwent a transformation from a collective nation of families and communities relying upon themselves and each other to fulfill the needs of individual societies, to a complacent and fractured body uncertain of the despotic nature of government and the extent to which the damage may be irreversible. When our citizens understand how government exploits our desire to fulfill our basic needs by manufacturing crisis, reason will inoculate us from such exploitation. The antithesis to rational ignorance, or the result of this inoculation should properly be referred to as "rational awareness."

The importance of an educated, well-informed society could not be understated in the goal to create and sustain rational awareness in the electorate. Our Founding Fathers understood this to be the case, as our society was the first in history to undertake the public education of the whole of society. Reflecting upon the sinister intentions behind the Stamp Act, Adams correctly identified how Statists first turn to the prevention of proper education. By preventing the "free flow of knowledge," despots attempt to withhold the intellectual means to discover their true intentions:

"But it seems very manifest from the Stamp Act itself, that a design is form'd to strip us in a great measure of the means of knowledge, by loading the Press, the Colleges, and even an Almanack and a News-Paper, with restraints and duties; and to introduce the inequalities and dependances of the feudal system, by taking from the poorer sort of people all their little subsistence, and conferring it on a set of stamp officers, distributors and their deputies."[109]

Adams offered insight to what consequences would be realized for allowing the press, bureaucrats, and public school employees who serve at the behest of their own interests to withhold truth and knowledge from our citizens:

---

[109] Adams, John. *A Dissertation on the Canon and the Feudal Law,* No. 4. Monday, 21 October 1765. *Papers of John Adams.* pg. 128 Edited Robert Joseph Taylor. Vol. 1. Cambridge, MA: Belknap of Harvard University Press, 1977

"Liberty cannot be preserved without a general knowledge among the people... They have a right, an indisputable, unalienable, indefeasible, divine right to that most dreaded and envied kind of knowledge — I mean, of the characters and conduct of their rulers."[110]

To what do we measure "the characters and conduct" of our leaders to if not for a moral law? Here in lays one of the dangers of secularization, which could be observed in Europe during the era of our Revolution. Secularization, to be sure, was a historical reoccurrence that could be observed and compared to the empires of Greece, Rome, Carthage and their mother England. It was obvious "the ancient republics" first displayed moral decay, which quickly followed an effort to reeducate the people in the laws of relativism. In the early republic, our Founding Fathers did take precautions to ensure that the American republic would forever recognize the everlasting and absolute Natural Law, which was created and is governed by our Creator, or the Laws of Nature and Nature's God as it is so beautifully written in the Declaration of Independence. If we are to sustain a society which measures "the characters and conduct" of our leaders and of ourselves to a worthy standard, then we live in a society that recognizes "the distinction between things just and unjust, made in agreement with that primal and most ancient of all things, Nature; and in conformity to Nature's standard are framed those human laws which inflict punishment upon the wicked and protect the good."[111] The Progressive Movement has demonstrates that we are not punishing the "wicked and protecting the good." For all of the progressive rhetoric, victories and promises, we have become a society which is far from just and closely resembles "democratic despotism." We have tried the progressive approach for the better part of a century and our political prosperity is in jeopardy, as is our very freedom.

In the following chapter we also will explore the Natural Law and its connection to the Creator. For the Founding Fathers, there could be no expectation to meet our obligation to sustain a just society if we do not understand whom it is to we are first and foremost obligated. It is necessary to examine the role of religion and morality in our society, what role religion was intended to play, America's religious history and how it has been a benefit to our society, and the negative stigma progressives have a attached to the church. As previously stated, blame is assigned where it is deserving of assignment, thus the blame for the decrease in church influence in society must ultimately be assigned to its leadership. Certainly government has taken measures to weaken church influence, and we will discuss them, but it is in times of persecution when church leaders are needed the most. We are to expect certain debauched behaviors from

---

[110] Quoting John Adams from Koch, Adrienne. *The American Enlightenment.* pg. 239 New York: George Braziller, 1965

[111] Cicero quoted from Ebenstein, William. *Great Political Thinkers.* pg. 135 New York: Holt, Rinehart and Winston, 1963

politicians, but not from church leadership, and they will not escape the deserved criticism they too often evade.

In the sections that follow, we will examine the natural deterioration of the family composition as a consequence of secularization and other social forces, as well as some of the many dangers which are of natural consequence, such as poverty and education. Past studies have covered empirical data concerning family composition, but no explanation has been provided, save anecdotal evidence. A psychological explanation will be provided in the context of Natural Law, and our natural desire to fulfill our basic and growth needs. The health of the family in society can serve as an indicator to political prosperity, as the cycle of family decomposition, poverty and violence, is irrefutable. The family is the bedrock upon which all societal strength is built; without it, there can be no political prosperity, and history proves that nobody understands this better than tyrants. It is the family from which all obligation to others is born, cultivated, and projected for the good of the whole of society and connectedness of human relationships. There was a time when this Natural Law was self-evident to Americans, and when viewed through the lens of human nature, it still is.

CHAPTER 3: VIRTUE IN SOCIETY

"Our Constitution was made only for a moral and religious people. It is wholly inadequate to the government of any other."[1]
John Adams

THE DECAPITATION OF CHURCH & STATE

The relationship between virtue and religion is consequential, that is to say, they are inseparably interwoven. To be virtuous, in practice, is to observe and obey the universal "Laws of Nature and Nature's God." Absent the acknowledgement of God, the obligation of one to care for the happiness of others becomes minimal. The only other reasonable alternative is a sense of duty to our fellow-countrymen, or patriotism. However, patriotism does not provide us with a doctrine of morality. There is no standard of right and wrong, or the sense of an authority to enforce or reinforce Nature's moral law. Patriotism, alone, always presents the danger that it can be misused to promote hyper-nationalism. Patriotism, was and is intended to compliment our obligation to God to care for the well-being of others, but cannot replace it. Anecdotal evidence, in the form of observation that a correlation exists between the secular effort to remove God from our public institutions and the waning of public virtue, is abundant in American society. The larger concern, however, is that we are becoming a people for whom the Constitution was not designed to govern. Progressives, to their credit, have long understood this to be the case. Thus, their push to a more secular society is actually an intentional effort to render the Constitution ineffective and unnecessary. In George Washington's farewell address, our Founding Father warned us of such a folly in thinking:

"Of all the dispositions and habits which lead to political prosperity, religion and morality are indispensable supports... And let us with caution indulge the supposition that morality can be maintained without religion... Reason and experience both forbid us to expect that national morality can prevail to the exclusion of religious principle."[2]

The words Washington chose to use – "indispensable supports" – refers to that which strengthens civil society, and "political prosperity" merely follows as a result. Virtuous *habits*, however, are too often overlooked as the true measure to

---

[1] Letter to the Officers of the First Brigade of the Third Division of the Militia of Massachusetts, 11 October 11th, 1798. Revolutionary Services and Civil Life of General William Hull. New York: D. Appleton & Co. 1848
[2] *Washington's Farewell Address.* Huszar, George B.; Littlefield, Henry W.; and Littlefield, Arthur W. *Basic American Documents.* Ames, Iowa: Littlefield, Adams & Co. 1953

limit government's necessity, and as such, are too infrequently practiced. The simple reason for this oversight, which is why we have struggled to sustain a sufficiently strong civil society, is that virtue must be taught through principled teaching of Natural Law. Washington, as did all of our prominent Founding Fathers, understood that religion and morality are the "indispensible supports" to a civil society that remains obedient and obligated to follow Nature's moral law. Minister and historian, Joseph Tracy, wrote *The Great Awakening* in 1842, in which he credited the 18th century religious revival for the American Revolution.[3] Although the colonies one-by-one joined in revolt against Britain for several reasons, their religion transcended all of them. More than any other element to American society it was our religion, especially the Protestant ethic, which shaped our culture.[4] Despite the enormous differences – both within and between the colonies – a common culture of values, ideals, and a general way of viewing the world was shared through the vehicle of religion.

The signing of the Declaration of Independence was, in itself, an act of obedience to the Laws of Nature and Nature's God. In signing their names, our Founding Fathers acknowledged that any manmade law that stands in conflict was, in truth, null and void. The opening of the Declaration reads:

"When in the Course of human events, it becomes necessary for one people to dissolve the political bands which have connected them with another, and to assume among the powers of the earth, the separate and equal station to which the Laws of Nature and of Nature's God entitle them,"[5]

While we read and pay lip service to the words in many of our founding documents, we fail to stop and put them in their proper context, which waters down their meaning. The Declaration of Independence, in essence, was a humbled repudiation of the strongest government on Earth, and a solemn pledge to God that they would obey and enforce His supreme universal laws. Natural Law dictates that humankind live in their natural state of freedom, that no government has the power to object to that freedom, and demands action against threats to liberty by those worthy of receiving it.

"But when a long train of abuses and usurpations, pursuing invariably the same Object [disobedience to the Laws of Nature and Nature's God] evinces a design to reduce them under absolute Despotism, it is their right, it is their duty, to throw off such Government,

---

[3] Tracy, Joseph. *The Great Awakening*. New York: Arno, 1969
[4] Middlekauff, Robert. *The Glorious Cause: The American Revolution, 1763 – 1789* Revised & Expanded Edition. pg. 51 Oxford University Press 2005
[5] *Declaration of Independence*. Brown, Richard D. *Major Problems in the Era of the American Revolution 1760 – 1791* 2nd Edition, pg. 170 University of Connecticut 2000

and to provide new Guards for their future security.[6]

Although the pretentious aristocratic class was weaker in the American colonies, nevertheless, our Founders lived in a society where political power came not from merit but birth, or the artificial aristocracy. The American merit-based society as we understand it to be was in a stage of infancy, which applied to economic mobility rather than political. Not surprisingly, in the colonies laymen assumed authority in churches of all denominations, which was representative of the American demand for equality in duty. The authority that justified the actions of subjects, whose motherland had already viewed as sub-standard second-class subjects, is found in the closing:

"And for the support of this Declaration, with firm reliance on the protection on divine Providence, we mutually pledge to each other our Lives, our Fortunes, and our sacred Honor."[7]

Considered enemies of the British Empire, facing certain demise if they were to fail in the efforts, they relied on the protection of God. When put into this context, or rather the correct context, the claims from Neo-Progressive historians, such as Charles Baird are ridiculous. Revisionist like Baird, have argued the Revolution was the product of the economic interests of a few wealthy Deists. For enemies of the State who did not believe in acts of God, they certainly profess a heavy reliance on God's protection. Our founding documents, and our Founders' personal correspondences written throughout the Revolution, suggest they were motivated by something much greater.

Whether or not the Founding Fathers held Deist beliefs does not contribute much to the discussion of the intended role that religion should play in society. First, there seems to be a general misunderstanding on what constitutes Deism. The constructive elements of Deism state that God exists, created the universe, and that His laws govern the universe. As was common in the Age of Enlightenment, Deists believe that God created human beings with the unique ability to use reason. Where Deism parts with traditional Theism is the belief that reason and the observation of empirical evidence in nature is sufficient enough to prove the existence of God. They reject most miracles, prophecies, and in most forms Deists discount the Trinity.

Skepticism surrounding the doctrine of the Trinity is to be expected from 18th century colonial Americans. They were the "children of the twice-born" who "despised the formality" of the established church; purest who followed the duty

---

[6] Ibid.
[7] Ibid.

of calling and lived by the Spirit.[8] Denominational Protestantism, although born in Europe, was grown to adulthood on American soil. The Catholic Church was, and remains to this day, under the centralized direction of a European Pope. Our Founding Fathers feared a transplanting of sorts from European to American soil, and along with it the papacy's centralizing power. Common among the colonists, especially in New England, was the suspicion of conspiracies being hatched by the Parliament under the corrupt influence of the Catholic Church. Pamphleteers bombarded their readers with accusations of sinister plots to enslave the colonies. The passage of the Quebec and Stamp Acts reinforced the concerns harbored and expressed by citizens in local taverns, preached of in sermons, and printed in activist literature. Parliament's efforts to reign in colonial obedience and pay for the French-Indian War, issues which seem irrelevant to the church, were in fact viewed by the colonists as an attempt to undermine religious liberty. Declaring the authority to breach the terms of colonial charters, coupled with the general willingness of Parliament to assert supremacy over colonial legislatures, made the idea more a logical conclusion than a wild conspiracy. Leading up to the Revolution, it became a dominant view that British constitutional government had already been corrupted, and their fellow-Englishmen deprived of their natural rights. The threat to liberty from moral decay among British rulers was of grave concern to our Founding Fathers, which should come as no great revelation to people whose forefathers fled England to preserve virtue, frugality, and the calling. Historian, Robert Middlekauff, describes the mood in the colonies:

"Where Protestant zeal burned fiercely and where the Catholic presence in Canada seemed ominous, the conviction grew that the threat against civil liberty posed by unconstitutional taxation was partly a papist conspiracy to subvert Protestantism."[9]

Second, the most notable figures of the Revolution who have been charged with holding Deist beliefs have expanded beyond the boundaries the evidence can corroborate. Thomas Paine, who was later imprisoned for his radicalism in France of all places, was not even an original signer of the Declaration of Independence. Benjamin Franklin, who documented in his autobiography his experimentation with Deism, claimed to grow wiser and older to the nature and behavior of the Creator. The events leading up to the Revolution, the outcome of the war itself, and the "spirit of cooperation" that followed, all served as evidence to Franklin that his earlier inclinations regarding the Deist doctrine were flawed.[10] In 1787, during the Constitutional Convention, he rose to speak on the

---

[8] Middlekauff, Robert. *The Glorious Cause: The American Revolution, 1763 – 1789* Revised & Expanded Edition. pg. 46 Oxford University Press 2005
[9] Middlekauff, Robert. *The Glorious Cause: The American Revolution, 1763 – 1789* Revised & Expanded Edition. pg. 131 Oxford University Press 2005
[10] Franklin, Benjamin. *On the Providence of God in the Government of the World.* 1730

subject:

"...the longer I live, the more convincing proofs I see of this truth – that God governs in the affairs of men."[11]

Thomas Jefferson, a frequent target for distortions by revisionists similarly exhibited Deist tendencies, which have drawn consider attention recently. Most notable, is his later work known as the Jefferson Bible. However, redacting passages that told of miraculous events was more a rebuke of the established church and less his disbelief in God's ability to do so. He referred to himself as a Unitarian, or one who believed that Jesus Christ was a great prophet, teacher, and in some cases the Son of God, but not God himself. As an early proponent of abolition, although a slave owner himself, Jefferson "trembled" from his belief that the sin's of slavery would be met with "supernatural influence," or divine intervention.[12] As he often did while reflecting back on the war, George Washington credited the success of the Revolution to divine intervention, and regarded the adoption of the Constitution as a justification from God. In a letter to the Marquis de Lafayette, Washington wrote:

"The adoption of the Constitution will demonstrate as visibly the finger of Providence as any possible event in the course of human affairs can ever designate it."[13]

There is no way to separate our founding principles from God's law. The debate over what public role the church would have in our new society was complex, contradictory, and varied by region. Among the vast number of sects, or denominations that migrated to the colonies, only the Anglican Church was established; if by loose requirements for dissenters to register, which were largely ignored could be considered established.[14] However, the discussion surrounded around the role each sect would play, not whether or not they would have one at all. The New England view advocated in favor of greater public support, and provided for the church in a way unheard of in modern progressive interpretations of an intended "separation of church and state." *The Massachusetts Declaration of Rights*, 1780, states:

"As the happiness of a people, and the good order and preservation of civil government,

[11] *The Records of the Federal Convention*, 1787. Edited by Max Farrand Vol. 1 pg. 451 New Haven: Yale University Press, 1966
[12] Quoted from Frazer, *Religious Beliefs of America's Founders*, p. 128 quoting Jefferson's *Notes on the State of Virginia*, 1800. p. 164
[13] *To the Marquis de Lafayette*, 7 Feb. 1788. *The Writings of George Washington*. Edited by John C. Fitzpatrick, Vol. 29 pg. 409 Washington: U.S. Government Printing Office 1931 - 1944
[14] Bailyn, Bernard. *The Ideological Origins of the American Revolution*. pg. 248 Cambridge, MA: Belknap of Harvard University Press, 1992

essentially depend upon piety, religion and morality; and as these cannot be generally diffused through a community, but by the institution of the public worship of God, and of public instructions in piety, religion and morality: the people of this Commonwealth have a right to invest their legislature with power to authorize and require, and the legislature shall, from time to time, authorize and require, the several towns, parishes, precincts, and other bodies politic, or religious societies, to make suitable provision, at their own expense, for the institution of the public worship of God, and for the support and maintenance of public protestant teachers of piety, religion and morality, in all cases where such provisions shall not be made voluntary."[15]

The controversial issue in the New England view was not the public funding being allocated to teach religion and morality, but the exclusion of faiths that were outside the traditional Congregationalist denomination. The "preservation of civil government" was absolutely dependent on "piety, religion and morality." In New England, the Congregationalists continued to receive public support well into the 19th century; however, strict "Separates" within the Congregationalist Church refused to accept any legal benefits provided for dissenters.[16] Benjamin Franklin wrote to the outspoken President of Yale University, Reverend Ezra Stiles, promoting the universal principles that all denominations and faiths could agree to promote publically:

"Here is my creed: I believe in one God, the Creator of the universe. That he governs it by his providence. That he ought to be worshipped. That the most acceptable service we render to him is in doing good to his other children. That the soul of man is immortal, and will be tested with justice in another life respecting its conduct in this. These I take to be the fundamental points in all sound religion."[17]

Ever the diplomat, Franklin underscored the debate between religious toleration and religious freedom. However, these were matters to be deliberated upon the individual state level. The difference in denominations was regional, which is to say, Congregationalists in New England and Anglicans in Virginia, and so on. The misinterpretation of the 1st Amendment by progressive federal courts is fundamentally flawed. The entire purpose for the Bill of Rights was to deny the federal government jurisdiction over codified states' rights, which obviously included religious freedom. The federal government was never intended to have the authority to force states to sever religious relationships. In 1787, the year of

---

[15] *The Massachusetts Declaration of Rights, Art III 1780.* Taylor, Robert J. *Massachusetts, Colony to Commonwealth.* Pg. 129 – 130 Chapel Hill, NC: University of North Carolina Press 1961
[16] Goen, C.C. *Revivalism and Separatism in New England, 1740 – 1800.* New Haven, CT: Yale University Press, 1962
[17] Franklin, Benjamin. *The Writings of Benjamin Franklin.* ed. Smyth, Henry A. Vol. 10 pg. 84 New York: Macmillan Company 1905 – 1907

the Constitutional Convention, the same legislative body passed The Northwest Ordinance. This outlined specific parameters that new governments northwest of the Ohio River, which must be republican in principle, would have to follow to gain entrance into the confederation of states. Again, we find a shared sense of necessity to promote the principles of virtue through basic religious tenets. Article III of The Northwest Ordinance blatantly reads:

"Religion, morality, an knowledge being necessary to good government and the happiness of mankind, schools and the means of education shall forever be encouraged."[18]

The idea of a "separation of church and state" was a distortion of Jefferson's rational; when as president he denied using his power to establish federally recognized religious holidays. Although Thomas Jefferson, the author of the Virginia Statute of Religious Liberty 1786, preferred equal status for all denominations he recognized the right of his neighboring to disagree. In his second inaugural address Jefferson said:

"In matters of religion, I have considered that its free exercise is placed by the Constitution independent of the powers of the general government. I have therefore undertaken on no occasion to prescribe the religious exercises suited to it; but have left them, as the Constitution found them, under the direction and discipline of state or church authorities acknowledged by the several religious societies."[19]

The consensus that emerged in our early republic was that religious principles are "indispensable supports" to the family, community, and necessary for the overall public welfare. In the vast majority of states no particular denomination was to establish dominance over the other, nevertheless, the state would promote, teach, and practice these universal principles. We know from observation that this debate was resolved to satisfaction by the 19th century. A national conviction that the tenets of morality and development of virtue were more important than differences between denominations, further developed into a national identity:

"The sects that exist in the United States are innumerable. They all differ in respect to the worship which is due to the Creator; but they all agree in respect to the duties which are due from man to man. Each sect adores the Deity in its own peculiar manner, but all sects preach the same morals laws in the name of God…All sects of the United States are

---

[18] *The Northwest Ordinance, 1787. Federal and State Constitutions: Colonial Charters, and Other Organic Laws of the States, Territories, and Colonies, Now or Heretofore Forming the United States of America.* Vol. 2 pg. 957 – 964 Washington DC: US Government Printing Office, 1909
[19] Jefferson, Thomas. *The Writings of Thomas Jefferson.* ed. Berg, Albert E. Vol. 3 pg. 378 Washington: The Thomas Jefferson Memorial Association 1907

comprised within the great unity of Christianity, and Christian morality is everywhere the same... There is no country in the world where the Christian religion retains a greater influence over the souls of men than in America.[20]

Not only was this education necessary to sustain public virtue, but the survival of our republic literally depended upon it. The practice of cherry-picking phrases that are then made to conform to a certain justice or justices' ideology, which are absent historical accuracy, deeply undermined our ability to instill in future generations these necessary values. Ignorant to the origins of traditional American ideals, such as freedom and equality, later generations became further and further detached from their identity and the historical truth. The secular push to redefine the meaning of the commonly heard phrase "separation of church and state," is the single biggest hoax perpetuated on *We the People*, which was designed to deliberately rob us of our American national identity.

Religion and American traditionalism have done more to further the promise of equality for all of our citizens than big government has ever or, ever will in the future, be worthy to receive credit for. Contrary to the progressive revisionist version of history, abolitionist sentiment was strong during the period of Revolution. The exclusion of citizenship for black Americans in our early republic was far from a consensus. Hamilton, Jay, Jefferson, Franklin, Washington and many others, all were opposed to slavery even though many at some point in their lives personally owned slaves. Washington, although upon his death provided for their release, would had done so prior if it were not for the legal restrictions and costs associated with emancipation. In 1794, out of concern that public knowledge would fracture the early republic, he quietly conspired to sell western lands to raise the money for emancipation.[21] Of the institution of slavery he wrote:

"...there is not a man living who wishes more sincerely than I do to see some plan adopted for the abolition..."[22]

Founders such as Franklin who belong to the former with Paine, and John Jay, Hamilton, and Burr who were members of the latter, frequented the Pennsylvania Abolition Society and the New York Manumission Society.[23] Their

---

[20] Tocqueville, Alexis de. *Democracy in America,* 1840. Vol. 1 pg. 314 New York: Vintage Books, 1945

[21] Higginbotham, Don. *George Washington Reconsidered.* pg. 127 – 128 Charlottesville: University of Virginia, 2001

[22] Quotes and Lafayette plans: Twohig, Dorothy. *'That Species of Property': Washington's Role in the Controversy over Slavery.* Higginbotham, Don. *George Washington Reconsidered.* pg. 121 – 122 Charlottesville: University of Virginia, 2001

[23] Kennedy, Roger G. *Burr, Hamilton, and Jefferson: A Study in Character.* pg. 92 New York: Oxford University Press, 2000

opposition to slavery was based on the principles of Natural Law, religion and morality, which were celebrated during the First Great Awakening. Although abolitionist sentiment was strong during the period of Revolution, the fragility of the early republic would allow the sins of slavery to go unpunished until it was at last indicted in the houses of God across our nation. The abolitionist movement exploded during the Second Great Awakening in the first half of the 19th century. Equality under God's law had demanded payment for the promise of liberty for all Americans; the promise of the American Revolution. William Lloyd Garrison, and later his followers Wendell Phillips and Frederick Douglas, all being products of the revival became "Holy Warriors" giving voices to the tenets of Natural Law. James Stewart wrote:

"All people were equal in God's sight; the souls of black folks were as valuable as those of whites; for one of God's children to enslave another was a violation of the Higher Law, even if it was sanctioned by the Constitution."[24]

The backward-thinking label, or the regressive stigma that religion and traditionalism have assumed in modern American society is simply inaccurate. It stems from the idea that somehow religion and widespread liberty cannot coexist. As with other Progressive Era ideas, this notion was not unique to America, but originated in the Statist-friendly venues of Europe. The parallels between the anti-religious wing of the philosophical movement in Europe, and the misguided academics that began in the Progressive Era and remain to this day, are nothing less than astonishing. The similarity arises from the belief among elites that religion, as a means of just order, is a foolish conviction held only by small-minded people. Furthermore, a church-centered culture strengthens civil society and reduces the need for dependence on the State for fulfillment of our hierarchy of needs. However, this is the historical tradition of America, which dominated society before the Progressive Era:

"The philosophers of the eighteenth century explained in a very simple manner the gradual decay of religious faith. Religious zeal, said they, must necessarily fail the more generally liberty is established and knowledge diffused. Unfortunately, the facts by no means accord with their theory. There are certain populations in Europe whose unbelief is only equaled by their ignorance and debasement; while in America, one of the freest and most enlightened nations in the world, the people fulfill with fervor all the outward duties of religion."[25]

---

[24] Stewart, James B. *Holy Warriors: The Abolitionists and American Slavery.* New York: Hill & Wang, 1976

[25] Tocqueville, Alexis de. *Democracy in America,* 1840. Vol. 1 pg. 319 New York: Vintage Books, 1945

The "Higher Law" has constantly challenged us to live up to our founding doctrines and, to ultimately right the wrongs that were reluctantly prioritized during the fragile, early period of our republic. Our faith and traditions have given us extraordinary strength through the enormous amount of tribulations, which Americans have been subjected to in an exceptionally short amount of time. The Third Great Awakening spiritually prepared Americans for the price we would have to pay for that promise on the battlefields at Bull Run, Shiloh, Antietam and Gettysburg; countless blood baths throughout the five very dark years that led to but didn't end in Gettysburg, Pennsylvania.

Despots fear the belief in God more than any other idea that can be shared among the ruled. There has never been a totalitarian state that has not, eventually, used their police powers to attack the freedom to worship one's own God. The despots, however, can hardly be the focus of blame for the secularization of America, as they are merely pushing social changes that have proven effective in the past. It is the job of the church and family to educate subsequent generations on duty of calling and the truth in Natural Law. The negative impact that secularization has had on social and political well-being is such that no one should escape culpability. The failure of church leadership to fulfill the traditional role of social leadership has become a significant detriment to the betterment of our society. During colonial times and well into the 19th century, the church leadership consisted of laymen who enjoyed no rich endowments, nor did they shrink at the task of leading their people against the grain of relative truth coming from despotic government. Sadly, in general, that is no longer the case.

The tax-exempt status pursuant to Section 501(c)(3) of the Internal Revenue Code demands that churches refrain from any participation or intervention in any political campaign for or against any candidate for public office, whether it is direct or indirect, and declares that the prohibition extend at least to oral and written statements supporting or denouncing a candidate.[26] I find no fault in church pursuit of tax-exempt *per se*, as there is precedent in both biblical and English common law texts. Regarding the latter, the history of English church tax exemption dates back to the Middle Ages, and runs right up to colonial America.[27] In the Age of Enlightenment, the rather correct rationale for exemption was that the church performed certain functions of a charitable and communal nature that the government could not perform.[28] Fact in point, even if it was in government's power they understood the dangers of promoting idleness. The church is in the unique position among the community to ensure

---

[26] 26 U.S.C. § 501(c)(3) (2007).

[27] Selborne, Roundell Palmer. *Ancient Facts and Fictions concerning Churches and Tithes*. pg. 36 London: Macmillan, 1888

[28] John Witte, Jr. *Tax Exemption of Church Property: Historical Anomaly or Valid Constitutional Practice?* 64 S. CAL. L. REV. 363, 369 (1991).

that assistance be provided without those in need abandoning their duty of calling. The Protestant ethic is ultimately what renders government-run welfare unnecessary and improper, thus it's under attack. However, by abandoning their own duty of calling, church leadership made feasible the prospect of having the ability to not just dilute but decapitate traditional virtues.

Prior to the establishment of a federal government, church-government relations in the American colonies reflected the diversity of sects in the colonies. Congregationalists detested establishment in any form, therefore, no duty performed by Adams' church bared a resemblance to the Anglican Church of Jefferson's youth. Uniformity came as early as 1802, when Congress provided a tax exemption for churches, which continued to exempt churches during the Civil War and after the passage of the Tariff Act of 1898.[29] The Progressive Movement gave rise to quiet voices that challenged 1st Amendment protections to all organizations afforded tax-exempt status. Although it was sold as an across-the-board consideration the vast majority of the organizations were faith-based. In 1934, Congress attempted to enact a ban on all political activity by tax-exempt organizations, but disagreement over the protection of charitable organizations led to a ban on lobbying alone.[30] The Progressive Movement pushes a philosophy of equality, but their definition requires reducing the abilities of both individuals and organizations, because they are powerless to increase the abilities of those lacking them. The misguided understanding of equality that does not distinguish between equality of opportunity and equality of ability, only serves to increase the suffering of those who might have benefited from the abilities of others. The Church has the willingness and capacity to provide certain services, which cannot be rivaled by other charitable and social welfare organizations with tax-exempt status:

"The fact that churches touch so many aspects of people's lives makes them different from other charitable and social justice organizations. A person might join Planned Parenthood or NARAL Pro-Choice America because they agree with one of the groups' position on abortion. They might even vote for a political candidate based on whether the candidate's views on abortion conform to their own and the groups' views. However, it is unlikely that either group will provide the range of social services, let alone the moral teachings, that churches provide."[31]

The existing ban on political activity for churches, in its current form, is solely

---

[29] Vaugh, James, E. *The African – American Church, Political Activity and Tax Exemption,* 37 Seton Hall Law Review. 371, 376 (2007).

[30] Houck, Oliver A. *On the Limits of Charity: Lobbying, Litigation, and Electoral Politics by Charitable Organizations under the Internal Revenue Code and Related Laws,* 69 Brooklyn Law Review 1, 23 (2003).

[31] Blair, Keith. *Praying For A Tax Break: Churches, Political Speech, And The Loss Of Section 501(c)(3) Tax Exempt Status.* pg. 413 Denver University Law Review May 19th, 2009

contributed to the political expediency of one of the most politically expedient politicians of the 20th century — Lyndon B. Johnson. Then-Senator Johnson faced a primary challenge from millionaire oilman, Dudley Dougherty. Backed by the conservative political group, the Committee for Constitutional Government, Dougherty favored restraining the treaty-making authority of the President of the United States; a winning issue in conservative Texas.[32] The conservative group printed material on the issue along with an endorsement of Dudley Dougherty. Under existing Texas law the endorsement was not permitted, however, the organization did nothing to violate existing federal law. While the amendment Johnson introduced was not precipitated by a specific conflict with a church institution, it was designed with the big government philosophy to monopolize social welfare organizations that limit government necessity, as well as suspiciously vague language. The desire to restrain church influence had deep roots in the Progressive Movement, but no politician could deliver the political muscle like the future "Great Society" designer. The restrictions outlined in Section 501(c)(3) apply to no other type of tax-exempt organization. Section 501(c)(3) defines a charitable organization as one that is:

"...*organized and operated exclusively for religious, charitable, scientific, testing for public safety, literary, or educational purposes, or to foster national or international amateur sports competition...or for the prevention of cruelty to children or animals...*"[33]

There are two concerns over the language and manner in which Section 501(c)(3) was written. First, it is evident by the language of the law that its design is to restrain organizations in support of civil society, or rather their ability to organize and influence their members to the benefit of the valuable services they provide. Progressives often make the erroneous claim that government intrusion would be unnecessary if civil institutions were sufficient, but government has actively blocked these institutions and those who support them from reaching their full potential. Second, the language of the law is arbitrary, which is why it results in its unjust arbitrary application. As to the first concern: why would the federal government not want to promote organizations that are in a better position logistically to be far more effective than government entities carrying out the social services mission? A civil society with a strong religious component is only a threat to a State that pursues a monopoly of social welfare services. Popular tyranny would consider the presence of civil society in the social welfare apparatus to be a double-edged sword. The potential benefits to the fiscal health of the State would certainly be desirable, as funds could potentially become readily available for special interest wealth-producing

---

[32] Houck, Oliver A. *On the Limits of Charity: Lobbying, Litigation, and Electoral Politics by Charitable Organizations under the Internal Revenue Code and Related Laws,* 69 Brooklyn Law Review 1, 24 (2003).
[33] 26 U.S.C. § 501(c)(3) (2007).

legislation; but the weight of the sword is one-sided indeed. The potential consequences outweigh the benefit to the extent that a civil society apparatus cannot simply be used to facilitate public services *per se*, but could facilitate a mobilization of popular support against tyrants and their special interest allies. Furthermore, from what we know of human nature, removing options to fulfill our needs drives us to be hungry "all over" with the desire to fulfill them, thus government exceedingly becomes the preferred avenue. Of course, all of these societal shifts are occurring simultaneously with the advancement of the ultimate goal, which is the removal of the empowering Protestant ethic from the American national identity.

Concerning the arbitrary pursuit of justice, specifically regarding churches, a recent example can be observed in the case of *Branch Ministries v. Rossotti*. Branch Ministries, Inc., had operated the Church at Pierce Creek in Binghamton, New York. Four days before the 1992 presidential election, the church ran ads in *USA Today* and the *Washington Times* entitled, "Christians Beware." The ad warned against Bill Clinton's positions on abortion, homosexuality and other social issues, which are contradictions to Bible scripture; therefore, they called on all Christian voters to vote against him. In the footer of the advertisement was a disclaimer informing the reader that the Church of Pierce Creek, as well as other unnamed churches and concerned Christians, had sponsored the advertisement. Along with this information was a mailing address to be used by those who wished to contribute to the cost of the advertisement. The *New York Times*, a progressive publication to be sure, jumped all over the churches' advertisement. On October 31st, 1992, an article on the front page blew the whistle on the church's plans to run the ad in 157 additional newspapers.[34] Within a month, which is incredible considering the federal government's typical reaction time, the Regional Commissioner of the IRS had informed Branch Ministries that he had authorized an investigation into the church, because he found "a reasonable belief...that you may not be tax-exempt or that you may be liable for tax."[35] Branch Ministries initially refused to comply, which promptly resulted in their loss of tax-exempt status. Following the revocation, Branch Ministries sued asserting a violation of the Religious Freedom Restoration Act of 1993. The church also claimed that the IRS engaged in selective prosecution, or arbitrary justice, which was in violation of the church's 5th Amendment's Equal Protection Clause.[36]

Rather than diving into the irrelevant weeds of whether or not every church is a religious organization under the law, which the court found them to be, the court held that "the sole effect of the loss of the tax exemption will be to decrease

---

[34] Applebome, Peter. *Religious Right Intensifies Campaign for Bush*. New York Times. A1 October 31st, 1992.

[35] Branch Ministries v. Rossotti, 211 F.3d 137, 140 (D.C. Cir. 1998).

[36] Ibid. pg. 141

the amount of money available to the Church for its religious practices."[37] The ruling, in and of itself, is arbitrary and represents how simple and often judges shape the law to meet the argument, instead of the argument satisfying the law. However, the statute ultimately allowed for such a ruling by the vagueness of its original design and language. Even academia has a difficult time reconciling the legal argument, although some may agree with the court's decision:

"However, the court appears to have taken the position that this loss would be irrelevant to whether the church could continue in its ministry. That view does not give enough weight to the effect of losing tax-exempt status. It is hard to imagine that a church would be able to minister to its congregants and provide pastoral care and services at the same level if the amount of money available to it were to decrease. Loss of the tax-exemption would directly impact how a church is able to exercise its religion."[38]

Despite the so-called logic, of course the loss of tax exemption is naturally detrimental to the church's ability to provide essential community services if not properly minister to their congregational members. It could be argued that the church should have simply not engaged in the political process in the first place, but that would not legally satisfy the 5th Amendment concern. Nevertheless, it could be concluded that ill intent is not present if the law is applied without selective, or arbitrary justice. Historically, or rather modern history, government has been arbitrary regardless of the motive, and it has undeniably served to benefit progressive tyranny and intolerance. Traditional churches that spread the ethic, duty of calling, true equality and virtue, are met with intolerance in the courts, the media and popular culture. On the other hand, radical social justice "religious" institutions, which comport with the progressive ideology, enjoy a very different standard of treatment:

"Barack knows what it means to be a black man living in a country and a culture that is controlled by rich white people."[39]

Those are the words of the now-infamous Reverend Jeremiah Wright, the once-senior pastor of Trinity United Church of Christ in Chicago, IL. His tenure at the radical church when then-Senator Barack Obama attended service, is well documented and not worth reiterating. But for the purpose of supporting the argument the ideology of the church, itself, is absolutely necessary to mention. The response to Branch Ministries was immediate by the progressive

[37] Ibid. pg. 142
[38] Blair, Keith. *Praying For A Tax Break: Churches, Political Speech, And The Loss Of Section 501(c)(3) Tax Exempt Status.* pg. 420 Denver University Law Review May 19th, 2009
[39] Sataline, Suzanne. Obama Pastors' Sermons May Violate Tax Law. *Wall Street Journal.* A1 March 10th, 2008.

establishment media, and the coverage prompted an unusual and immediate government response. Admittedly, it would be fair to label the *Wall Street Journal* conservative, although it is a fact the publication segregates hard news from editorial opinion, it still is true that the revelations of Reverend Wright did not come out for years after the activity was documented. It is also true, however, that the IRS acted in a minimal capacity to appease public opinion, and no attempt to revoke the tax exemption status of Trinity United Church of Christ was made. Whereas Branch Ministries defended traditional positions found in the Protestant ethic, and in the Christian Bible for that matter, Reverend Wright is a student and mentor of Black Liberation Theology as founded by James Hal Cone. Unlike traditional American Protestant rivals, which gave birth to events predicated on the idea of equality as the Revolution and abolition movements were, Cone invented a new divisive Christian theology that focused more on oppression than liberation. The philosophies of Black Liberation Theology are compatible with the progressive ideology, as neither deals in absolutism. As the needs of the State evolve, for Cone, so should it be with theology:

"We cannot solve ethical questions of the twentieth century by looking at what Jesus did in the first. Our choices are not the same as his. Being Christians does not mean following in his steps."[40]

In other words, they must bend their convictions to reconcile them with their cause, rather than the cause being the result of their convictions. Black Liberation Theology would have found no home in the historical abolitionist movement, as it is nothing more than social retribution masquerading as "social justice"; the two are now, if they weren't always, one in the same. It rejects absolute truth in favor of theoretical flexibility to reconcile scriptural inconsistencies and historical inaccuracies. Cone incited a generation of black Americans with selective historical interpretations, which concluded that "unless white America responds positively to the theory and activity of Black Power, then a bloody, protracted civil war is inevitable."[41] Yet, Black Liberation Theology conveniently omits the historical culpability of West African kings who, in reality, "proved remarkably adept in accommodating European demands for captive labor with their own control of the long flourishing internal trade in slaves."[42] Nevertheless, religions of relativism are of little concern or threat to the State. In fact, they can prove quite useful for their ability to incite crisis. It is worth mentioning, as well, unlike

[40] Cone, James H. *Black Theology and Black Power* (20th Anniversary Edition) pg. 139 New York: Harper, 1989
[41] Ibid. pg. 143
[42] Historical Statistics of the United States: Colonial Times to 1970. pg. 1168 Bicentennial Edition. Washington D.C., 1975 and Middlekauff, Robert. *The Glorious Cause: The American Revolution, 1763 – 1789* Revised & Expanded Edition. pg. 32 Oxford University Press 2005

the traditional ethic, Cone preached victimization. Cone frequently equated the struggle of the black community with the Exodus, however, Moses wanted no reparations or retribution from Pharaoh, nor did he expect to judge Pharaoh lest he be judged himself by God. Furthermore, Moses and the Israelites lived by a code of absolute law, unchanging and everlasting. The Israelites wanted nothing but to be free to enjoy autonomy in the promise land, and had they not been forever surrounded by hostiles, to live and let live. Cone, however, was right regarding oppression of black America, but he had directed fault at the wrong community. Preachers of Black Liberation Theology, corrupt community leaders and progressive politicians, all play a role in denying black Americans the autonomy they deserve. Recently, Project 21 and other groups have emerged with the mission to dismantle these oppressive societal barriers, but for now, these influences help to explain why black Americans are "a major exception to the significant correlation between religiousness" and the denouncement of progressivism.[43]

Religion and private education apparatuses, which have the potential to prevent or even overcome rational ignorance among the electorate, are clear targets in the language of the statute. Minorities, specifically black Americans, are indispensable to the progressive coalition, and as such, the government arbitrarily allows certain churches to violate the prohibition on political activity. Of course, government is acting predictably according to Natural Law when it exhibits aggression against civil society, but the behavior of church leadership is contributing to the decline in congregational participants across America, as well.

Aside from the evident violation of 1st Amendment protected rights, it is also a violation of church leaders' duty of calling to speak on political and social issues with their congregations. Church leadership, however, do not seem to be taking their obligation all that serious in the modern era. On October 2, 2011, as part of Pulpit Freedom Sunday, out of the 450,000 churches in the United States only 539 conservative Christian pastors made what can be classified as political statements.[44] The Alliance Defense Fund is a Christian legal fund that is dedicated to defend clergy from legal action against the progressive secular watchdog groups who threaten action in federal courts. The 2011 effort was an extension of the groups 2008 Pulpit Initiative, in which a mere 33 pastors found the education of principle to be a worthy burden to bare. There has been cause for optimism, as the following year brought 84 pastors to the cause, and the following 100, and so. However, as a matter of sheer statistics, it is an inadequate participation rate for us to expect a significant impact on the public. It seems that church leaders are less concerned with their calling and more concerned with the

[43] Newport, Frank. *Gallup: Seven in 10 Americans Are Very or Moderately Religious but Protestant population is shrinking as "unbranded" religion grows.* December 4th, 2012
[44] Birky, Andy. *Few Consequences Currently Faced by Pastors Who Endorse from Pulpit.* iowaindependent.com, October 6th, 2011

preservation of the status quo – and Americans know it.

Since 1973, there has been a clear long-term decline in Americans' confidence in church institutions. From its high of 68 percent in 1975, confidence in American churches has plummeted to 44 percent in 2012, which strongly coincides with the loss of church influence among the American people. In 1957, 69 percent of Americans saw religion increasing its influence in society. By 2010, that number had fallen by 44 percent to 25, even as 75 percent now say more religion in society would be positive.[45] Both the data from public opinion studies, as well as the actual empirical observations of the decline in traditional institutions, suggests American church leaders have a significant disconnect.

A study conducted by the Pew Forum on Religion and Public Life, found that evangelical Christian leaders in the Global North are significantly more pessimistic than their counterparts in the Global South regarding the outlook for evangelical Christianity. While 71 percent of church leaders in the Global South expect the state of evangelicalism to be "better than now," only 44 percent in the Global North agree.[46] In the United States, a majority of evangelical leaders – 53 percent – view the state of evangelicalism worse than the previous 5 years; 48 percent expect it to worsen still. The deep divide stems from the leaders' opinions of themselves, how to change the negative perception, and the causal factors for the deteriorating status of the church. By 92 percent, American church leaders in the United States overwhelmingly view secularization as a major threat to evangelical Christianity, which may explain the relative pessimism compared to leaders in the Global South who do not by such a majority. But secularization is closely followed by consumerism and popular culture, specifically sex and violence. All of those considerations are valid, but the American people are more concerned with issues of hypocrisy and immoral behavior from the church in past decades. From 1973 – 1985, "the church or organized religion" was consistently the most highly rated institution in the Gallup confidence in institutions measure, outperforming even institutions in the United States military and the U.S. Supreme Court.[47] The descent in confidence occurring in the mid-late 1980s coincided with the scandals involving televangelist preachers Jim Bakker and Jimmy Swaggert. Just as confidence in organized religion began to recover during the late 1990s, scandal rocked America's other large institution when charges of child molestation by Catholic priests rocked the confidence index, bottoming it out at the then-low measure of 45 percent.[48] The scandal itself could only be shadowed by the subsequent cover-

---

[45] Newport, Frank. *Gallup Study: Near-Record High See Religion Losing Influence in America*. Dec. 29th, 2010. See also Saad, Lydia. *Gallup: U.S. Confidence in Organized Religion at Low Point*. July 12th. 2012.

[46] Unless otherwise specified all data on church leaders was collected in study by Pew Forum on Religion and Public Life: Global Survey of Evangelical Protestant Leaders. June 22nd, 2011.

[47] Saad, Lydia. *Gallup: U.S. Confidence in Organized Religion at Low Point*. July 12th. 2012.

[48] Ibid.

up engaged in by the members inside the ranks of church leadership.

The church leadership in America has yet to come to terms with the fact that they have failed to earn back the trust of the American people. Instead of viewing church failures as a threat to the future of the Christianity, the vast majority finds fault in outside influences. As a whole, only 30 percent of those interviewed reported "leading lavish lifestyles" as a major threat to the future of evangelical Christianity, which juxtaposed to the traditional view in the Protestant ethic of worldly asceticism bares little resemblance. Perhaps reflecting that Protestant sects remain conscious of the Catholic sex scandals, 43 percent of U.S. church leaders view violations of sexual morals as a major threat, compared with only 23 percent from other countries.

There have been numerous studies to show personal religious sentiment among Americans has actually begun to arrest the upward trend toward secularization. However, if a mere acknowledgement of the existence of God was sufficient to realize the documented benefits to religious observation, then we should not experience the damage we have to our traditional institutions i.e., family composition, civil society, etc. The willingness of Americans to keep God in their hearts and beliefs, yet failing to live in the Spirit, is a reflection of failure by church leadership. Although all of the empirical data hints at a certain inconsistency, majorities in both the Global North and South see a natural conflict between being an evangelical and living in modern society, and this is even truer of the church in the United States. Worldwide, 64 percent believe the conflict to exist, whereas in the United States the figure increases to 71 percent. However, our modern government is increasingly secular, yet church leaders are so willing to cede ground to a hostile institution. While progressives have been tirelessly working to transform social institutions into something that is unrecognizable from a traditional American institution, only 16 percent of evangelical Christian leaders see the task of reforming institutions as their duty as a member of church leadership.

The vast disconnect between how Americans view the church and how the church views themselves is reminiscent of the same "artificial aristocracy" that plagues government institutions. The American people perceive much of organized religion as a vehicle for ambitious individuals to achieve their ends, which more likely than not can explain public skepticism over the prospect of a closer relationship between religion and government.

It is inconceivable that Jonathan Mayhew, Pastor of the West Church in Boston, would have refrained from delivering his sermon on the anniversary of the execution of Charles I; in which he asserted that resistance to a tyrant was a "glorious" Christian duty.[49] Preaching moral sanction for political and military resistance, Mayhew articulated the position that most ministers took during the

---

[49] Mayhew. Jonathan. *Discourse Concerning Unlimited Submission and Non-Resistance to the Higher Powers.* Boston: D. Fowle and D. Gookin, 1750 Library of Congress (83)

conflict with Britain; that civil and religious liberty was ordained by God. The
most important political parson of the American Revolution, John Witherspoon,
would not have been present in Philadelphia to sign the Declaration of
Independence had he refrained from professing his political views. Theodore D.
Weld, William Lloyd Garrison, Arthur and Lewis Tappan, all were the products
of preachers like Lyman Beecher. Beecher, Nathaniel Taylor, and Charles G.
Finney stressed each person's responsibility to uphold their obligation to God in
society. Sadly, progressive social justice preachers have perverted the moral
imperative preached during the Second Great Awakening, which for the time
being is still useful to the despotic cause. Progressive special interest continues to
fight to diminish influence of church leaders and church tenets. Despite the rich
history of positive effects in the 17th – 19th centuries, many of these groups wish
for no religious element to remain in America society. It is equally inconceivable
to imagine what the 20th century would have looked like with respect to civil
rights had Reverend Dr. Martin Luther King Jr. not engaged the political
process. As Pastor of Dexter Avenue Baptist Church, Dr. King organized the
Montgomery bus boycott. As a result of Rosa Park's refusal to give up her seat on
the bus, the Supreme Court ended segregation in public transportation.[50]
Reverend King's methods, as well as other leaders who followed him in
furthering the cause of civil rights, were not limited to protests while abstaining
from the political process. Politicians sympathetic to the civil rights movement
were the beneficiaries of church mobilization at the ballot box, and church
leaders mobilized church members:

*"There can be little doubt that the 'church' and the teachings of the 'church' played a
prominent role in Reverend King's leadership and in the lives of the thousands who
participated in the civil rights movement because of him. It is not overstating the issue to
say that the modern civil tights movement would not have been successful were it not for the
support of Reverend King's church and other black churches."[51]*

Almost 300 years have passed since the founding of the Massachusetts Bay
Colony by the Puritans. The movement of colonists to New England, known as
the "Great Migration," was predominantly of families who held a vision of a new
society, not just economic opportunity, but a "Shining City upon a Hill."[52] The
Puritans created a deeply religious, socially tight-knit and politically innovative
culture, which is still present within modern Americans. They hoped this new

[50] Kirk, John. *Martin Luther King Jr.* pg. 19 – 36 London: Pearson Education Limited, 2005 see also:
Brenman, Marc. *Transportation Inequality in the United States: A Historical Overview.* 34 HUM. RTS.,
Summer 2007
[51] Blair, Keith. *Praying For A Tax Break: Churches, Political Speech, And The Loss Of Section 501(c)(3) Tax
Exempt Status.* pg. 411 Denver University Law Review May 19th, 2009
[52] Winthrop, John. A Model of Christian Charity. Sermon written on board the Arbella in 1630.

land would serve as a "redeemer nation." They fled England and in America attempted to create a community designed to be an example for all of Europe. The mothers and fathers of our Founding Fathers fled to America to escape the immorality of Europe in search of religious liberty, and their children spilt their blood in obedience to God to preserve it. But now, we have regressed against Natural Law for the false promise of "progress."

FAMILY DECOMPOSITION

Republicanism is the product of real world observation regarding human relationships. Duty, understanding, and affection between citizens are stronger in society when the relationships are personal. In the simplest of terms, we care more about people we intimately know, therefore, we respond out of obligation to their needs. If a person needed money for the needs of their child, the protection of property or any other necessities to fulfill the basics in their hierarchy of needs, they wouldn't seek out assistance from an unfamiliar relationship, nor would they expect to receive it. As humans, we turn to those who are most intimate with the happenings of our lives. There is no other communal relationship that instills in us a greater obligation than the one between families. It is for this very natural reason that the family must be the foundation of any free society, as it is our natural supportive unit in society by natural design. *Political Prosperity*, which in reality is a product of a strong civil society, is unattainable unless the family composition remains strongly intact.

Beginning in the middle of the 20th century, progressive ideological movements have produced intentional social forces that have resulted in the weakening of America's family composition. Progressive feminists, who must be categorized in their own right considering progressives are not at all the whole of the feminist movement, began challenging the traditional family as the nest from which personal growth is nurtured. Much of this agenda has been pursued in an anti-nationalist capacity, utilizing the United Nations to support same-sex marriage, the pro-abortion position, and government support for child care so that women may pursue careers.[53] Ironically, progressives preach collective action over individualism, yet we observe here that self-interest is clearly placed above the well-being of the whole of society. The connection between family composition and poverty, education and violence, have not deterred progressives from emphasizing the importance of what they promote as diversity, even though the damage caused by family decomposition discriminates against no identity.

Popular culture aided the transition in the mid 20th century, as one study

---

[53] Wilkins, Richard G. The United Nations, Traditional Family Values, and the Istanbul Miracle. pg. 123 – 144 Selection from Proctor, Scot. Charting a New Millennium. Salt Lake City: Aspen Books, 1998

points out how this "shift is illustrated by the movie *Pleasantville*," in which the traditional American family is portrayed as a structural barrier to personal growth.[54] Politicians beholden to the entertainment industry share a good deal of culpability, as do church leaders who would rather trade the absolute truth of Natural Law for relevance in the modern era. Of course, the intended end of this transformation is not diversity, or some enlightened modernism meant to "progress" society further toward a more just society, it is the eradication of absolute truths and morality. The selfish needs of government and its allies are ever-changing, and such as the case with the Protestant ethic, stability and autonomy which derives from a belief in morality and traditionalism leaves little opportunity for exploitation of needs. Unfortunately, as a result of the progressive agenda we have experienced a decline in morality, which has occurred simultaneously with a decline in traditional American family composition. Thus, it should come as little surprise to see a simultaneous rise of societal irregularities.

In 1964, a full 93 percent of children born in the United States were born to married parents. Subsequent to the "Great Society" reforms, we have seen a sharp decline in child births to married parents; in 2010, just 59 percent.[55] As will be discussed in the following section, child poverty is one of the most tragic results of progressivism, as marriage decreases the probability of child poverty by upwards of 82 percent.[56] Marriage, along with education, are extremely effective at combating poverty, but one must nurture the other. In the section following poverty, we also discuss how the studies of school choice programs illustrate how ineffective the laws of men are at coercing good parental behavior, thus the need for virtue, morality and other tenets of the ethic. But what other consequences can there be for individuals, or even if we consider the whole of our communities, if we continue to lightheartedly ignore the health of Nature's basic communal unit and our own obligations.

Absentee fathers, and even those who are physically present but do not meet their parental obligation, have allowed the disease of poverty to become an epidemic. In fact, 75 percent of non-married fathers continue to carry on an intimate relationship with the mother at the time of birth, but they are far less likely to abuse drugs, alcohol, or the mother physically.[57] The lack of commitment can only be explained by the change in social norms as a result of the progressive agenda, such as the one previously mentioned, which encourages fathers to shirk their obligation by fulfilling the basic needs of both the mother and child. The traditional prerequisites demanded by society in large part no

---

[54] Heaton, Tim B. Social forces that imperil the family. pg. 20 Dialogue. 32, (4).

[55] Rector, Robert. *Marriage: America's Greatest Weapon Against Child Poverty*. Special Report # 117 on Poverty and Inequality. The Heritage Foundation. September 5th, 2012.

[56] Ibid. Unless otherwise specified.

[57] Rector, Johnson, Fagan, and Noyes. *Increasing Marriage Would Dramatically Reduce Child Poverty.*

longer exist, and as Peck argued, it is in our nature to avoid problems as long as we find the alternative acceptable to our basic needs.

"Even though they aspire to remain together, most unmarried-parent couples also fail to understand the role of commitment to successful relationships. In the real world, all relationships have stressful and trouble periods; successful couples have an enduring commitment to each other that enables them to weather difficult periods and emerge with stronger, happier relationships. In our culture, such strong commitment to a relationship rarely exists outside of marriage. Because they fail to understand the importance of commitment, most unmarried-parent couples tend to fall apart when they hit difficult periods that are inevitable in all relationships."[58]

Worth noting, as well, is that with the Protestant ethic comes the obligation of parents to God to take "the road less traveled," or do what is right although it may be difficult. Peck's thesis is validated not only by our innate common sense, but the study of human behavior in a "feel good" welfare society. Unfortunately, while this might generally seem acceptable to one or both of the parents, the development from childhood to adolescence and adulthood for the child proves a vicious cycle, indeed. Society, as a whole, sadly overlooks our children's growth needs, or the need to be loved and possess self-esteem. This is where the idea that government can supplement civil society is ultimately proven a farce. Government may be temporarily capable of fulfilling the basic needs of the child through food stamps, housing, etc., but is it impossible for government to meet our growth needs. In fact, the very social welfare policies by which the basic needs of the child are met, are the same policies responsible for the absence of the very person the child needs for personal growth; and, if education is effective at combating poverty, then the obligation of fatherhood is paramount to the child's well-being. Children born to single parents are far "more likely to have emotional and behavioral problems; be physically abused; smoke, drink, and use drugs; be aggressive; engage in violent, delinquent, and criminal behavior; have poor school performance; be expelled from school; and drop out of high school."[59] The absence of the natural and morally validating means of fulfilling our growth needs can mean all of the difference between healthy and unhealthy behavior; success or failure; happiness or misery; and ultimately, freedom or tyranny.

Perhaps, the greatest folly of progressivism is that both purists and despots are

---

[58] Rector, Robert. *Marriage: America's Greatest Weapon Against Child Poverty.* Special Report # 117 on Poverty and Inequality. The Heritage Foundation. September 5th, 2012.

[59] Ibid. from Manning, Wendy D. and Lamb, Kathleen A. *Adolescent Well-Being in Cohabiting, Married, and Single-Parent Families.* Journal of Marriage and Family, Vol. 65, No. 4 (2003), pp. 876–893. Data from Add Health study. See also Dawson. *Family Structure and Children's Health and Well-Being: Data from the 1988 National Health Interview Survey on Child Health.*

misguided enough to believe they will be the exception to Natural Law. That is to say, at least some of them truly believe they can "fundamentally transform" America into the first stable "feel-good" society; in which, everything is relative so long as it comports with the modern age it shall be deemed acceptable behavior for society. I am often struck by how historically naïve this supposition truly is, as if such an "accomplishment" would be unique. Immorality, relativism, secularism and arrogance in the face of traditionalism, are actually the historical norm. Whereas, the pursuit of virtue and obedience to Natural Law has made America the anomaly. Our Founding Fathers saw "elegance, luxury, and effeminacy begin to be established" and later looked back with the understanding that their "frugality, industry, and simplicity of manners, would have been lost in an imitation of British extravagance, idleness and false refinements" had they not revolted.[60]

On the other hand, perhaps the greatest folly of conservatism as it relates to the American family is that their perception of the perfect "Ozzie and Harriet" home is mostly an ideal creation. Instead of living by the principles of virtue they profess, they condemn those whom only God can condemn, if He so chooses to do. Nevertheless, a strong family composition has always been the foundation of America's political prosperity. By comparing American families with the families of Europe, Tocqueville observed:

"There is certainly no country in the world where the tie of marriage is more respected than in America, or where conjugal happiness is more highly or worthily appreciated. In Europe almost all the disturbances of society arise from the irregularities of domestic life. To despise the natural bonds and legitimate pleasure of home is to contract a taste for excesses, a restlessness of heart, and fluctuating desires. Agitated by the tumultuous passions that frequently disturb his dwelling, the European is galled by the obedience which the legislative powers of the state exact. But when the American retires from the turmoil of public life to the bosom of his family, he finds in it the image of order and peace. There his pleasures are simple and natural, his joys are innocent and calm; and as he finds that an orderly life is the surest path to happiness, he accustoms himself easily to moderate his opinions as well as his tastes. While the European endeavors to forget his domestic troubles by agitating society, the American derives from his own home that love of order which he afterwards carries with him into public affairs."[61]

While the importance of the family is often dismissed and its natural order mocked, the empirical data to be discussed in the following section from this ignorance are irrefutable. Tocqueville, in essence, was describing Europe's social

---

[60] Wood, Gordon S. *The Creation of the American Republic, 1776 – 1787.* pg. 110 Chapel Hill NC: University of North Carolina Press, 1969
[61] Tocqueville, Alexis de. *Democracy in America,* 1840. pg. 315 Vol. 1 New York: Vintage Books, 1945

problems to be the cause of its political dysfunction. The European powers were burdened with debt, their economies in malaise, as waning production struggled to keep up with the promises made by progressive politicians misguided by progressive philosophies. The observation of Natural Law combined with the call for frugality, or worldly asceticism, and the natural satisfaction of being content with the products of your labor were abandoned in Europe. In America, our contentment came from the wholeness that could only be found in our family, but we have repeated the same tragic mistake made by 19th century Europeans. Both our fiscal and political prosperity has struggled to accommodate the "irregularities" in our domestic lives. Family composition is an effective combatant against poverty, violence, and even more important, provides an environment that is more conducive to a child's studies.

POVERTY, THE ETHIC, & THE HIERARCHY OF NEEDS

There are few issues that are more effective at exposing the progressive redistributionist ideology as the false promise it is, than the issue of poverty. No economic system can lay claim to the amount of people being lifted up out of poverty and destitution, than free market capitalism. Despite the appealing class warfare rhetoric of the Marxist ideology, no nation practicing its redistributionist policies has ever or, ever will, rival the diversity of prosperity that our nation has enjoyed. However, other capitalist countries in Western Europe have not duplicated America's success in a free market economy, either. The reasons for which we have been bestowed this blessing will be examined in this section.

European nations, whom of which it is a stretch to classify as capitalist economies, have been markedly more secular than the United States. When Weber arrived in the United States in 1904, his experience was an affirmation of his earlier thesis in the *Protestant Ethic*. In June of 2003, almost 100-years later, an article in the *New York Times* observed:

"Many scholars have built careers out of criticizing Weber's thesis. Yet the experience of Western Europe in the past quarter-century offers an unexpected confirmation of it. To put it bluntly, we are witnessing the decline and fall of the Protestant work ethic in Europe. This represents the stunning triumph of secularization in Western Europe — the simultaneous decline of both Protestantism and its unique work ethic."[62]

The *Protestant Ethic* did indeed celebrate its centennial by "achieving the status of verity."[63] As surprising though it may be to find such a commentary in a

---

[62] Ferguson, Niall. *The World; Why American Outpaces Europe (Clue: The God Factor)*. The New York Times. June 8th, 2003.
[63] Ibid.

publication of the *New York Times*, even this observation is incorrect in its assumption that secularization is a new phenomenon of the "new" Europe. Progressivism took hold in Europe much earlier than we have seen in America. Perhaps, the proximity of neighboring Eastern Europe's socialist countries facilitated the proliferation of collectivism. At the time the aforementioned article was written, 48 percent of Western Europeans reported attending church almost never, and the average of Northern Europeans who said God was a non-issue in their lives was 52 percent.[64] In a Gallup study conducted one-year later, only 9 out of the 25 member countries of the European Union had at least one-fifth of the adult population report to participate in weekly religious activities.[65] The plague of idleness from which the European Union suffers is further exacerbated by the lack of Protestant influence. Estonia and Latvia, the Baltic countries in which an element of Protestant tradition can still be found, are among the more severely secularized in the Union, with only 4 percent and 7 percent reporting weekly attendance.[66]

Capitalism, as with any other economic system to include socialism, does result in inequalities. The presence of economic inequality in any economic system is unavoidable. Any argument to the contrary exposes our naïveté to matters of economics, history, and the psychology of human behavior. The most preferential economic system acknowledges such realities and promotes civic work-duty to every able-bodied member of society. When the vast majority of citizens are answering their calling to labor we reduce the power among those who create economic disparity. The logical and proven means of accomplishing productivity is to offer incentive, or rather to give the individual the means for social mobility, above all being private property rights. As individuals fulfill their hierarchy of needs, the capability of the whole of society to empower others grows, as well.

Proponents of modern conservatism have a tendency to advocate laissez-faire without conceding structural restrictions exist for certain citizens. If it is the case that these restrictions are nonexistent, then how is it the progressive ideology manages to resonate within certain communities? Poor Americans have more housing space, products of leisure, and overall access to bare necessities than does the average citizen living in Western Europe. But in some ways, juxtaposing the experiences of poor Americans with those in other countries leaves out a basic element to human psychology. Michael Tanner put it best in one of his many works on American poverty, when he wrote that the "starving child in Somalia may not be aware of all that he is missing, but the poor child in America is."[67]

---

[64] Ibid.
[65] Manchin, Robert. Religion in Europe: Trust Not Filling the Pews. Gallup September 21st, 2004
[66] Ibid.
[67] Tanner, Michael. *The End of Welfare: Fighting Poverty in a Civil Society.* pg. 6 Washington: Cato Institute 1995

While it is true that America offers more opportunity for class mobility than most western countries, there is and has been, a growing number of citizens who feel entrenched in their economic station. To advance the conservative movement and address poverty, the two being continent upon each other, respecting and comprehending the psychology of poverty is imperative. The national discussion needs to begin with a mutual agreement that this is an economic reality for many of our citizens. Only then can we move forward. Identifying the cultural and structural restrictions on class mobility that cause poverty has largely been accomplished. Cultural restrictions, however, get trapped in that cage of political correctness and are altogether ignored. It is in the cultural element that we can comprehend the psychology. Until the discussion shifts to an honest dialogue that includes our societies' inconvenient truths, the progressive agenda will remain the dominant approach.

This is problematic, because whether it is intentional or not, progressivism perpetuates the cycle of poverty. Unions, bureaucracies, social workers, physicians, and other organized special interest who have a vested interest in the design of poverty programs, ensure the implementation of policy benefits them regardless of the programs' stated intention.[68] Our approach has been to outsource our societal obligation to those who find little financial incentive to address cultural restrictions or empower others to meet their hierarchy of needs. For them, it is practical and profitable to make poverty comfortable, and to a certain extent consistent. Indeed, this has been the reality of poverty since President Johnson declared "war."

Progressive arguments disproportionately focus on the inequalities of rights, prejudices, and other social justice themes. This is very effective at garnishing political support, which is no doubt the intention, but does little to combat the root causes of poverty. The enormous amount of data provided by public and private sector studies identify family composition, education, wages and work rates, as all being major contributors to poverty. The cycle of poverty is just that, a cycle. Events that self-perpetuate can present a problem when attempting to find the source, or rather the old "chicken or the egg" question. However, poverty is one of those issues where the data and common sense are all intertwined. Both suggest that only one of the major contributors – family composition – is a cultural and root cause of poverty. Government spending on education, vocational training, healthcare, and housing, are after-the-fact efforts designed to combat structural restrictions to social mobility. Statistically, as we will soon explore, traditional family composition is a prerequisite to overcoming these restrictions. Does it make sense for investors to continue to fund a venture that has a flawed business model? The answer is simple, but this is what society

---

[68] Lee, Dwight R.; & McKenzie, Richard B., *Failure and Progress: The Bright Side of the Dismal Science.* pg. 120-22 Washington: Cato Institute 1993

continues to do when our tax dollars are transferred to government funded programs to combat poverty.

Consider the Brookings Institute study conducted by Ron Haskins and Isabel Sawhill, the results of which, Haskins used to testify in front of the Senate Finance Committee for purposes of policy prescription. The study found that children of single-parent households are over four times as likely to grow up in poverty than children who are raised in two-parent households.[69] In 2009, the poverty rate among children in married-couple families was 11.0 percent, compared to children under single-parent (mother only) households, which is 44.3 percent.[70] The fact that studies utilized for the purpose of policy determination measure the single-mother households and not single-fathers is another telling inconvenient truth, which the policy refuses to acknowledge. Nevertheless, considering the increase in children living in female-headed households, it is logical to expect any government action would include policy directed at reversing this trend. From 1950 – 2010, the percentage of children living in single mother households has climbed from 6.3 percent to 23.9 percent.[71] In Figure 3.1, we can see the almost parallel relationship between the overall poverty rate and those within single-mother households.[72] The sheer number of children living within single-mother households causes the upward pressure on the poverty rate. Absent government assistance, the reduction in poverty would be an astonishing 25 percent if only our society experienced the same divorce rate that occurred during the 1970s.[73]

The recommendations put forth in the Brookings study calls for more government assistance to treat the symptoms with no consideration to the cultural restrictions on social mobility. They do, however, raise the concern that the increase in single-parent households has become an overwhelming challenge for the government, and likely offsets gains that might have been made as a result of massive government spending. But unfortunately, the suggestions put forth are aimed at saving the government money, not educating our citizens on societal obligation. Providing access to birth control or funding mass media campaigns to encourage males to use condoms may be cost-effective to the government, but there is no evidence that this will discourage the problematic behavior. Unless society is educated on the causes of poverty, and feels a moral obligation to the children whom they threaten to expose a life of hardship to, such policies will only serve to encourage irresponsibility and dependence.

---

[69] Haskins, Ron & Sawhill, Isabel. *Creating an Opportunity Society.* The Brooking Institute, Washington D.C. 2009

[70] Ibid.

[71] U.S. Census Bureau, Families and Living Arrangements, "Table FM-1: Families by Presence of Own Children Under 18: 1950 to Present" 2010

[72] Figure 3.1

[73] Ibid.

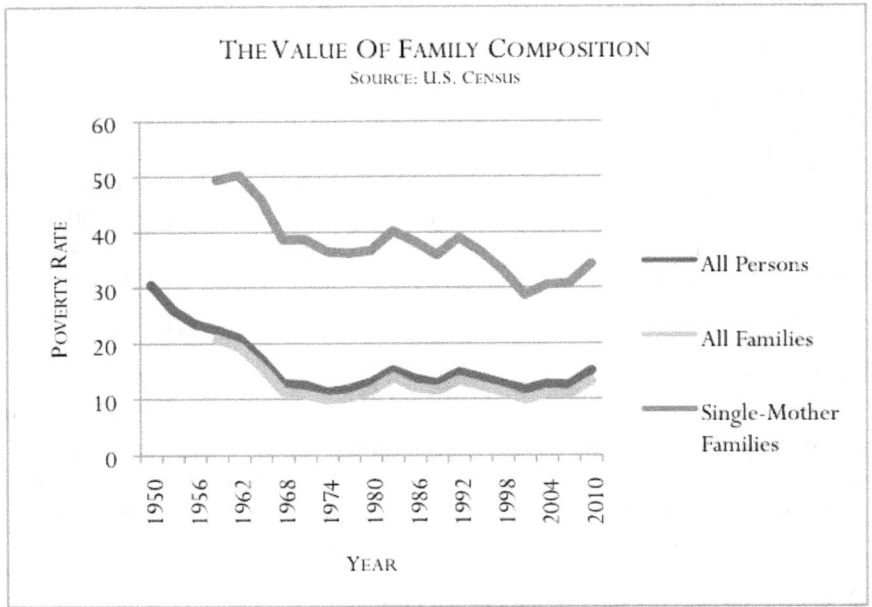

THE VALUE OF FAMILY COMPOSITION
SOURCE: U.S. CENSUS

All Persons

All Families

Single-Mother
Families

YEAR

Figure 3.1: We can clearly observe the rapid precipitation in the poverty rate prior to Lyndon B. Johnson declaring "an unconditional war on poverty in America." Furthermore, we can easily conclude that "Great Society" policies have perpetuated poverty and sanctioned fatherlessness.

The conservative claim that government assistance encourages dependency is either ignored by policymakers, scholars, and the like, or met with feverous resentment. However, the best kept secret among the elite circles is that there are groups that provide us with empirical evidence to make such a claim. Common sense would seem to dictate as much, but since these examples do not fit the narrative designed to promote the progressive agenda, they are hidden from the public discussion.

Since President Lyndon B. Johnson declared "an unconditional war on poverty in America," there have only been two periods of significant reductions in the poverty rate, relative to a decade prior. In the 1980s, when President Reagan actually reduced government spending as a percentage of GDP, and again in the late 1990s.[74] From 1983 – 1989, poverty declined to 12.8 percent, reversing much of the 33 percent increase under the Carter administration, which set the rate at 15.2 percent. Prior to Johnson's "war," the poverty rate was plunging and sat at 19 percent at the time of his State of the Union speech on January 8th, 1964. Despite the increase in government spending on welfare assistance programs, the poverty rate has remained flat with unappreciable bumps

---

[74] U.S. Census Bureau, Families and Living Arrangements, "Table FM-1: Families by Presence of Own Children Under 18: 1950 to Present" 2010

up and down. Amidst bipartisan criticism over the AFDC, or Aid to Families with Dependent Children, President Clinton had campaigned on the promise to reform welfare. Beginning in the late 1980s, most notably with Republican governor Tommy Thompson in Wisconsin, state programs had begun to reform and restrict welfare eligibilities. Following the "Republican Revolution" in the 1994 mid-term elections as part of the "Contract with America," increased pressure on the federal level finally led to the passage of the Personal Responsibility and Work Opportunity Act of 1996.[75] The bill included provisions that returned autonomy to the states, reduced federal welfare subsidies, and put in place a work component for recipients.[76] In addition to the work component, which is a manifestation of a belief in the calling to work, the "faith based initiative" of the 1996 welfare reform act recognized that churches are necessary providers of services, such as food banks, job counseling, and general delivery services to the community at large.[77] The progressive pressure, which resulted in Clinton twice vetoing prior conservative proposals, lessoned as poverty and welfare participation declined. Naturally, economic growth contributed to the reduction in unemployment, but prosperity coupled with the encouragement to pursue social mobility decreased dependency. Declines in welfare caseloads were reflective of normal economic growth, but we didn't begin to see a rapid decline until the reforms were enacted.

Welfare reform teaches us three important lessons. First, progressives will always oppose policies that empower individuals, even if they are effective. President Clinton would never have signed welfare reform unless the American people politically forced him to do so. They have had a considerable amount of time to reconsider their position. Incredibly, not only have they not rescinded the original predictions of doom, they have been successful in loosening the key work provision, as it is an extension of the effort to eliminate the American work ethic identity. Logic and reason can only lead one to suppose that dependency is indeed the objective. Second, is the importance of private sector dominance over the public sector. Recipients were successful at finding work, but they can only stay off of the welfare caseloads permanently if the private sector remains strong enough to offer continued opportunity.

The third lesson speaks to the conservative claim that welfare creates dependency. The bill was representative of the remaining Protestant ethic element within American society, as the work component is confirmation of a belief in a calling to work. It has always been an American instinct to avoid

---

[75] Reference to the 1994 mid-term elections that led to the first Republican majority in 40 years. The Contract with America included welfare reform as part of a legislative platform promised to the American public during the campaign.

[76] Personal Responsibility and Work Opportunity Reconciliation Act of 1996, Pub. L No. 104 – 193, § 104(A) and (B), 110 Stat. 2105.

[77] Ibid.

idleness, as for most, idleness creates unhappiness and unproductive behavior. This is clearly the general case. The decline beginning in 1994, represents those recipients for whom the promise of economic mobility was sufficient to motivate them into the workforce. The steeper and even more dramatic decline after the work provision kicked in demonstrates that some recipients, in general, needed additional motivation. For many, they felt little or no obligation to the federal government or taxpayers whom they had never met. In order to feel an obligation to break the cycle of dependence, individuals must feel an intimate need to do so, as is the case in our families and communities. There can be little doubt that the retention rate in the workforce was in part due to the dignity of being self-reliant. Certain aspects to human psychology exist, which the law and data are wholly insufficient to capture. There is a great deal of confidence and optimism deserved to human behavior, which progressives refuse to acknowledge, nurture, and promote lest they lose power. Welfare reform demonstrated that once empowered, an individual will strive to fulfill at the very least, the basics in their hierarchy of heeds. In an article in March 2006, Haskins wrote, "Welfare reform has been a triumph for the federal government and the states – and even more for single mothers."[78]

Consistent with tenets and ideals of republicanism, the federal government being the most distant in relation to the individual citizen could hardly rely on a sense of obligation to drive civic work-duty. That is why the work component was so vital and the law so successful. The need for legal compulsion is less the closer the human relationship becomes, although the effectiveness of legal compulsion is ultimately limited. However, the direct relationship between the federal government and the citizen is less an empowering partnership and more a parental trust. A perfect example of autonomy and empowerment leading to community reliance and obligation, are the Lumbee of North Carolina. The rampant destitution that plagues Native American communities is comparable to the worst of urban poverty.

What this evidence underscores is the importance of the third element to citizenship, and more specifically, societal obligation or the citizen-to-citizenship relationship. Government programs are not designed to increase social mobility so much as they are to redefine the relationship between the citizen and the State. Socio-economic equality is always the stated goal, but never the end result. The reason for this phenomenon is that assistance programs are intended to create a direct relationship between the citizen and the State. This not only encourages government reliance and relegates citizens to a life of dependence, but also has been instrumental in eliminating a citizen's societal obligation. Traditional reliance on family and community for the welfare of the individual is severed. Absent the element of intimacy, we dehumanize our society and make it easier to

---

[78] Haskins, Ron. *Welfare Reform, Success or Failure? It Worked.* Policy & Practice. pg. 12 The Brookings Institute Washington D.C. 2006

relieve our citizens of their obligations to themselves and each other. This causes a basic disconnect in our human relationships, with cultural restrictions falling by the wayside during the discussion.

In caring for our health we practice preventive medicine, because the data and common sense show that it is more effective and less costly than treating the symptoms of an ailment. In the same fashion, common sense should dictate our society's reaction to the causes of poverty. Government policy is directed at treating the symptoms of poverty rather than the root cause. Furthermore, at first glance, there seems to be an element of illogical policy application. That is to say, it makes little sense to pay someone else to do a job that we could do at the community level, and for less. However, when we understand human behavior, especially as it relates to the work of Peck, the honest answer is in our natural tendency to avoid our problems. It is easier to defer the problem of poverty to a third-party, or in this case the government, because it is difficult and we are distracted by our own economic situations. Civil society requires obligation, which of course requires a sustained effort, and that is not an easy task. Yet, it is not impossible, as the progressive argument would have us believe. There are those who value virtue and freedom above convenience; and, they are rewarded with social and political prosperity.

THE EDUCATION VACCINATION: INOCULATING AGAINST RATIONAL IGNORANCE

As America moves farther and farther away from our proven principles, there remains what some may find to be an unlikely community in North Carolina that has kept those principles alive. This section tells the story of the North Carolina Lumbee Tribe in the context of a specific issue that affects all Americans today – education. It is, indeed, a story worth telling; a story that needs to be told; a story that will remind us that the solution to America's failed education system is not that distant, after all.

The enormity of America's challenges are clearly flustering politicians, and demoralizing our citizens. Our leaders are lost and haven't the first clue how to fix our broken education system, or revive the American economy – two issues that are interrelated. The Lumbee, on the other hand, are composed of communities whose education model is both thriving and improving; but this wasn't always true. In 1835, the North Carolina State legislature passed laws that prevented Indians from voting, owning and using firearms, and took a general position to keep the Lumbee people downtrodden and weak. For a 50-year period, the Lumbee people experienced a generational loss of education. In 1885, the North Carolina General Assembly allowed the Lumbee Tribe to establish a "separate but equal" school system. With $500 and every able-bodied individual, the tribal community came together to build and establish the Croatan Indian Normal School; now known as the North Carolina University of Pembroke.[79] By the end of the 19th century, the tribe had established schools in 11 of their principle settlements.

Reliance on state assistance has always proven inadequate to meet the hierarchy of needs for the Lumbee Tribe, and it was no different when it came to providing proper education to their children. Tribal leaders donated private land and provided private funding to meet the community's educational needs. Every member of the community was expected, but never needed coercion, to play a role to meet the demands of their people. Today, schools throughout the Lumbee school system greet over 6,000 students at their doors each year - much of them of other races. In the 1950s, the foresight and wisdom of the tribal leaders resulted in outsider regulations to loosen - allowing whites and others to become absorbed into the Lumbee Tribe. The faces within Lumbee society have too changed, but unlike America, the principles remained the same.

The secrets to the success of the Lumbee Tribe, and the failure of other Indian nations, are tucked away in the pages of history. The Indian Removal Act of 1830, which was signed into law by President Andrew Jackson – the racist founder of the Democratic Party – did not remove the Lumbee Tribe from their native lands. Although persecuted, as a result the tribe did not have to forfeit their plenary power to the federal government. The parental relationship between the government and other Indian nations sapped the strength of Indian family composition. The ability to acquire ownership of land allowed the Lumbee Tribe to accumulate wealth through risk taking, or by leveraging that land.[80]

The infamous "Trail of Tears" destroyed other Indian nations' family structures, and those who did arrive with the family unit intact were unable to enjoy such autonomy, which is the foundation of empowerment. Such is the nature of government, they failed other Indian nations by failing to live up to their parental "trust responsibility." Of course, this should come as no surprise, as Natural Law dictates that no State power can supplement for the power and obligation of the family and community, which are the true and natural foundations of our society.

The Lumbee have lived with the government as a partner, not a parent. They have made education a responsibility and obligation for the family and community to meet, as did our Founders. As we look at the relationship between the modern school system and the government, the only partnership is between them, with American parents assuming a childlike role under the parent government. Teacher Unions and politicians have effectively undermined

---

[79] Interviews with the Lumbee Tribe Public Relations Department and
http://www.lumbeetribe.com/index.php?option=com_content&view=article&id=123&Itemid=34
[80] Ibid.

empowering parental and community obligation. In North Carolina, Lumbee Tribe communities have actually assumed responsibility to meet the hierarchy of needs of white, black, and other races in close geographic proximity to their communities.

The highly autonomous Lumbee of North Carolina exemplify the natural superiority of American traditionalism and principle. As Americans "progress" passed the need to obey the Natural Law, a church is a stone's throw away from every public or charter school in every Lumbee community.[81] Their communities emphasize a reliance on family to meet their hierarchy of needs, which is consciously pursued as a policy by the Tribe's autonomous leadership. They have never succumbed to the politics of victimization, despite having a history of oppression, and not never let the disease of hate and resentment pass on to their children. As American children ages 13 - 18 are suffering addiction, teen pregnancy, record illiteracy rates, record drop out rates and exhibit bankrupt morals, Lumbee parents proudly register their children for civic programs, such as Teen IMPACT. The mission statement for the program reads:

"Teen IMPACT promotes personal development through youth volunteerism. Our non – school based volunteer club, engages tribal youth ages 13 – 18 in meaningful community services, while enriching the understanding through peer support, mentoring, and service learning."[82]

Empowerment of the individual, family and community, was always an American principle. Coupled with traditional morals, obligation and civic duty, Americans can still rebuild a strong civil society that is capable of meeting the hierarchy of needs in our communities. Turning our back on these fundamental American principles for the false promises of big government, or rather relying on a "trust relationship," will be a tragic mistake for America to make. Indeed, it will be a tragic mistake for humanity. Education for the Lumbee Tribe is approached in the same manner and with the same principles as every other need in American life. We recognize an essential service and devise ways to meet the needs of that service's demand. If we find a productive and effective method to meet those demands, then we compete, and this competition forces us to evolve into ever-better providers; except in the case of education. The government monopoly will vehemently and even violently oppose any other community organization – public or private – who may have a better way to meet those demands, even if it means sacrificing the education of our children.

In 2013, the Oakland school board voted 4 – 3 to board up three of the highest-performing schools in the state of California. Ben Chavis, Lumbee Tribe

---

[81] Ibid.

[82] http://www.lumbeetribe.com/index.php?option=com_content&view=article&id=188&Itemid=83

member and former head of the American Indian Model charter schools, was the target of the government monopoly of the education apparatus. There is not, and has never been, any charges of impropriety filed against Mr. Chavis, except the unsubstantiated allegations made by government officials, which were only used to eliminate competition from AIM charter school. In the process, the students who were hurt the most from the decision were the very students that the progressive agenda claims to regard a priority – minorities. Commenting on AIM in his 2011 study, Andrew Coulson claimed:

"I found that AIM is the highest-performing charter school network in the state, by a wide margin...Low-income black and Hispanic AIM students actually outperform the statewide averages for wealthier whites and Asians. AIM even outperforms Lowell, one of San Francisco's most respected and academically selective high school."[83]

School choice programs empower parents to choose which schools – both public and private – they wish their child or children to attend, utilizing the public funds that would have otherwise been appropriated to union dominated public schools, despite performance. Coulson called it a "tragedy to deny current and future generations the opportunity to attend these schools."[84] Naturally, the unions are concerned with their inability to evolve and improve the education they provide, because they cannot compete with the quality provided by Chavis and the American Indian Model charter schools. Progressives, incredibly, regurgitate the same arguments against school choice, and advocate for the government monopoly education system. Public education is a failure, and if the education of our children is not important enough to overcome selfish ambition in the pursuit of wealth and political power, then the state of our union is worse than can even be described. Nevertheless, we will address some of the emotionally charged arguments put forth by the progressive-backed unions, and compare those claims with the facts.

Proponents of the government monopoly of the education apparatus in America are well-funded in their opposition to the policy of school choice, and as a result, only 250,000 students nationwide attend private schools outside that powerful apparatus.[85] The legislative battle is typically waged in the public arena, which the media then pushes with five traditional talking points. They, progressives, claim that school choice has a negative impact on the actual academic outcomes of choice participants, or the students and their families; school choice has a negative impact on the taxpayer-funded public schools themselves; will have a negative fiscal impact on taxpayers, or whether or not

---

[83] Coulson, Andrew J. *OUSD Made Wrong Decision to Close American Indian Charter Schools.* CATO Commentary, March 26th, 2013.

[84] Ibid.

[85] *The ABCs of School Choice.* Friedman Foundation for Educational Choice, 2013 edition.

school choice ultimately costs more than the government monopoly; predictably, school choice will facilitate an increase in racial segregation in schools; and ironically, school choice undermines American democracy. The argument, itself, has changed little over the last two decades, but the empirical evidence has mounted against the progressive argument:

"A large body of empirical evidence examines these questions using scientific methods. Twenty years ago, before this body of evidence existed, there was some excuse for making policy based on speculation, anecdotal observation, and intuition. Today, the effects of these programs are known, and there is no longer any excuse for policymakers and opinion leaders to be ignorant of the facts."[86]

Currently, there are 41 school choice programs in 22 states and Washington D.C., from which researchers can draw empirical data for the purposes of determining the viability of prior progressive arguments.[87] The first progressive claim, or supposed concern that school choice will have a negative impact on student performance, would ironically be unnecessary had the government monopoly not failed to produce satisfactory academic outcomes. Nevertheless, the argument claims that school choice will siphon off the higher ranked students into private schools, leaving the lower ranked students in a failing public school system. Public schools will become increasingly unable to educate the students left behind, as the funding will no doubt be considerably smaller than the private schools. It is often referred to as the "blob," or the bloated bureaucracy, as "draining money" and "creaming students." This argument is valid, that is, if you calculate potential outcomes using a government-centered approach instead of a free market-centered approach. In total, there have been 12 such empirical studies, which have examined academic outcomes, or student performance for school choice participants using random assignment. It is imperative that the studies utilized the random assignment technique when comparing student performance, which is considered the "gold standard" of social science, because any empirical data observed through random assignment are attributed to the education system and not the individual students. By randomizing treatment assignment, the group attributes for the different treatments will be roughly equivalent; therefore, any effect observed between treatment groups can be linked to the treatment effect, and is not a characteristic of the individuals in the group. Of the 12 studies conducted, 11 found that choice improves student outcomes, including 6 in which all students benefited, and five in which some benefited and some were not affected. Only one study found that no visible

---

[86] Forster, Greg. *A Win-Win Solution: The Empirical Evidence on School Choice.* pg. 3 The Friedman Foundation, April 2013.

[87] *The ABCs of School Choice.* Friedman Foundation for Educational Choice, 2013 edition.

impact could be observed, but no empirical study observed a negative impact.[88]

On demographics, the alternative approach that uses what is known as "matched" samples, has compared the experience of similar high school students in Milwaukee to either validate or contradict the findings found using the random assignment approach. The School Choice Demonstration Project, or SCDP, found that voucher students were more likely to graduate High School, attend college following graduation, and more likely to stay in college than their "matched" public school counterparts.[89] Interestingly, although progressives immediately turn to demographics for popular talking points, the one control that this approach cannot account for is one factor that progressive policies discourage – parental motivation.

The impact of school choice has a clear benefit to the performance of the students, but what of the impact on the schools themselves? Increasing student performance across the board is no doubt a success, but long-term success is certainly contingent upon the long-term stability of our educational institutions. Since 2011, there have been 19 empirical studies that have examined school choice's impact on academic outcomes in public schools; of which, 18 found school choice to have a positive impact, but the one study that found no impact was conducted on a school choice program that was specifically designed to insulate public schools from the program, itself.[90] The empirical data must justifiably include all methods when studying the consequence or benefit of school choice on public schools. Unlike the study of student performance, there are no variables for individual characteristics that present methodological barriers to overcome i.e., parental motivation. It is significant that results by region are uniform, that is to say, the results from Florida public schools mirror Wisconsin in unanimity. No state study found the doom and gloom predications of "draining money" and "creaming students" to be valid. In fact, one theory that arose from the study conducted in Florida proposed the contrary. Instead of "creaming" the best students, school choice actually "dredges" the students that performed the worst. To be fair, the Friedman Foundation study conducted by Greg Forster, noted that 9 studies of the Florida voucher program directed at underperforming schools found that the mere threat of eligibility for voucher enrollment improved those schools, rather than the presence of a dredging effect.[91] He supports the free market-based claim by citing the fact that a number of studies followed students individually, "rather than whole schools and still found that school

---

[88] Forster, Greg. *A Win-Win Solution: The Empirical Evidence on School Choice.* pg. 3 – 9 The Friedman Foundation, April 2013.

[89] Joshua Cowen, et.al. *Student Attainment and the Milwaukee Parental Choice Program: Final Follow-Up Analysis.* School Choice Demonstration Project, Report 30, February 2012.

[90] Forster, Greg. *A Win-Win Solution: The Empirical Evidence on School Choice.* pg. 11 – 13 The Friedman Foundation, April 2013.

[91] Howell and Peterson. *The Education Gap.* pg. 61 – 65; and Wolf, et. al. *Evaluation of the D.C. Opportunity Scholarship Program.*

choice improves outcomes for students who remain in public schools."[92]

If the data from studying the impact of school choice on students and schools reveals to us anything of importance regarding the nature of citizen-to-government relationships, it is that government cannot coerce societal obligation. In this case, of course, the societal obligation is of the parent to their child or children, which the studies refer to as parental motivation. Parental motivation must be a control in the studies of school choice on student performance, and it is wholly irrelevant to measure when studying school performance. But policies of empowerment, not replacement, incentivize parents to engage in their obligation to their child's education. While this clearly benefits the children, who are receiving a competitive education, at the same time parents are growing in themselves. The necessary reforms that schools must undergo in order to meet their "customers'" demands, fulfills the needs of three different groups in our society simultaneously; the students need for an education, the parents need to meet their obligation to their children, and the assurance of our schools proper function. Will meeting these needs have a negative fiscal impact on taxpayers?

Although the federal government has such a major role in education, public money spent on education from the federal government is only approximately 10%. Therefore, the only significant and measurable fiscal impact from school choice comes from the state level, which accounts for roughly 47%.[93] In total, 6 empirical studies have examined school choice's fiscal impact on taxpayers, and all 6 found that school choice saves money for taxpayers. The majority of federal funding allocated for education is conducted under Title I, which deals with low-income students based on demographics, and the remainder of the funds are appropriated for special-education programs. For the aforementioned reasons, implementing a nationwide school choice policy could realistically enable the federal government to again operate in its proper role as outlined in the Constitution – which is no role, at all. The simple concept of having the money follow the student as opposed to the student following the money, results in the lowering of cost through competition, as well as the promotion of parental motivation.

The under-acknowledged area of success for the progressive ideology in academia, the media and popular culture, is racial politics. The politics of division which are so closely identified with the progressive ideology serves not only to ensure political success, but the policies are actually used to sustain that success; as well as prevent good public policy from being implemented. The absurdity of the widespread charge that school choice facilitates segregation is even more ridiculous than the defense of the unacceptable *status quo* regarding student

---

[92] Forster, Greg. *A Win-Win Solution: The Empirical Evidence on School Choice.* pg. 12 The Friedman Foundation, April 2013.

[93] Digest of Education Statistics, 2011 edition. National Center for Education Statistics, 2012, table 180.

performance. The public school system of government monopoly is practicing, at this moment, a policy of racial segregation. Public schools are segregated by race in their current form, as the students in the public school system are assigned to a school based on where they live. Sadly, as the data proves, progressives either vehemently oppose or outright ignore the only viable solution for overcoming these residential barriers, school choice. In *Freedom from Racial Barriers: The Empirical Evidence on Vouchers and Segregation*, Forster has documented the effort to disallow the proliferation of the truth regarding the residential restriction embedded into the government monopoly.[94] There have been 8 empirical studies that have examined school choice and its impact on racial segregation in schools. Of these 8 studies conducted, 7 found that school choice moves students from more segregated schools into less segregated schools, and 1 found no net effect on segregation from school choice.[95] Despite the politics of racial division, which in part explains how black America defies the correlation between religion and rightward political thinking, there has yet to be one empirical study conducted that has found school choice increases racial segregation.

Progressive studies that demonstrate increased segregation have a flawed tendency to compare grade levels that are not the same. The problem with this method is that elementary schools tend to be more segregated than secondary, or post-elementary schools, because elementary schools assign students from smaller geographical areas. When a study is conducted by comparing schools to the racial composition of the greater metropolitan area as a whole, then researchers are privy to a greater degree of segregation than studies that focus on an individual district. The 1 study that found no net effect to segregation was conducted as part of the School Choice Demonstration Project. Tracking individual students from school to school, they found that both the private and public schools in the greater Milwaukee metropolitan area were both segregated. However, students switching from public to private schools and visa versa did not significantly impact the racial composition of either.[96] It is important to note the change in the racial composition of the area. In 1994, when the U.S Department of Education began to track the racial composition of private schools, Milwaukee private schools were overwhelming white – 75%; but by 2008, the same metropolitan private school composed of only 35% white participants.[97] What this can tell us is that school choice, despite race or region, demonstrates how the principles of free markets ultimately do apply to K – 12 education:

[94] Greg Forster. *Freedom from Racial Barriers: The Empirical Evidence on Vouchers and Segregation.* Friedman Foundation for Educational Choice, October 2006.
[95] Forster, Greg. *A Win-Win Solution: The Empirical Evidence on School Choice.* pg. 19 – 21 The Friedman Foundation, April 2013.
[96] Greene, Jay; Mills, Jonathan; and Buck, Stuart. *The Milwaukee Parental Choice Program's Effect on School Integration.* School Choice Demonstration Project, Report 20, April 2010.
[97] Woodworth, James and Forster, Greg. *The Greenfield School Revolution and School Choice.* pg. 20 Friedman Foundation for Educational Choice, June 2012.

"One thing the voucher program facilitated was the creation of new private schools that are predominately minority, so it is possible that segregation levels were always equal between public and private schools, and the voucher program simply shifted some of the heavily minority segregated schools to the private sector. Still, the large shakeup in both sectors suggests it is at least as likely that old barriers may have been broken down."[98]

As far as undermining democracy, it appears it isn't so much the democratic system itself that concerns progressive proponents of the government monopoly, but rather the outcome of the democratic process. Whereas the descriptive method is used to measure segregation due to its relevance in capturing racial composition, and random assignment is used to capture the effects on student performance, measuring civics and values requires a more comprehensive approach. Random assignment is a rather small pool of studies, in fact, the last publication was released in 2002. The descriptive comparison was made in only one study of San Francisco's voucher program, in which no impact was measurable. However, this study could justifiably be excluded, because it is literally the only study conducted with the descriptive method. The research in this case is much more field specific, where researchers generate hypothetical questions to pose to students meant to reflect tolerance of specific societal groups, political issues and the right of others who may disagree with their own to hold and practice those beliefs. For instance, upon identifying students' least desirable group, they are then questioned on whether or not they should be permitted to enjoy the same status in society as those who agree with their own beliefs. If, for example, Christians are identified as said group, the students are then asked if Christians should be permitted to have a Bible in the public forum, such as a library.

David Campbell conducted the latest nationwide study in 2013. Regarding political tolerance, utilizing random assignment, school choice participants were found to score higher, but on knowledge of civics, the data are less conclusive.[99] Although this study shows some positive impact, random assignment leaves out a critical element, which may be irrelevant to the performance of schools, but not with respect to civics – the family. However, the two recent studies conducted by David Fleming, and presented to the American Political Science Association in 2012, did include data that are useful in measuring the potential impact of school choice on the civics of parents, as well . After all, the role of the family in society is of the utmost importance to the overall health of society; and as such, has far-reaching consequences in many more areas than education, alone. Fleming's

---

[98] Forster, Greg. *A Win-Win Solution: The Empirical Evidence on School Choice*. pg. 20 The Friedman Foundation, April 2013.

[99] Campbell, David. *The Civic Side of School Reform: Private Schools, School Vouchers and Civic Education*. unpublished manuscript, provided by the author via email to Greg Forster on January 24, 2013.

study found that the effect of school choice as it relates to civics, is positive on both the students and the parents. The parents, empowered by being in charge, are much more likely to engage with their children's education. They join, or attend parent-teacher groups at much higher rates than non-school choice parents. School choice parents were much more likely to report a connection between the importance of education and what could be considered traditional civic institutions. According to school choice parents, the role and example is not lost upon the children, whom of which are found to involve themselves in civic duties at a higher rate when they take an interest in learning the nature of government.[100]

Overall, including the variations in methods, 7 empirical studies have been conducted on school choice's impact on civic values and practices, such as respecting the rights of others and the understanding of civic knowledge. Of the 7 studies conducted, 5 found that school choice improves civic values and practices, and 2 found no visible impact from school choice. Yet no empirical study has found that school choice has had a negative impact on civic values and practices. Progressives and their allies, to be sure, are concerned with these results and their evident benefits to society. However, it is a concern for its potential to disrupt the *status quo*, which threatens the bureaucratic and union power structure. Instead, they accept the fact that that which keeps them in power, rational ignorance, has certain negative productions, such as poverty and that which comes with poverty – violence.

TARGETING EMPOWERMENT & THE RIGHT OF PROTECTION

Perhaps, there is no more appropriate issue to end our discussion on the impact of virtue in society, than the 2nd Amendment. The modern era, which is one with the erroneous image of guns as depicted in news and entertainment, admittedly presents a challenge to educate the public on the many aspects of the 2nd Amendment. The consequence of public ignorance on this issue as dictated by Natural Law, is grave. The right of the citizen to defend themselves against tyrannical government is an essential right of protection for free people. The 2nd Amendment is often misunderstood in its reason for existence, as well as the realities of life when it does not exist. A thorough examination of media bias reveals how, for years, the media has underreported instances of appropriate gun usage. Whenever the 2nd Amendment is used for self-defense, "mums the word" in the state-run media.[101] This effort, by which bias is used as a tool to convince

---

[100] Fleming, David. *Privatization, Political Learning and Policy Feedback.* paper delivered at the national conference of the American Political Science Association, August 30-September 2, 2012.
[101] Lott, John. *More Guns, Less Crime: Understanding Crime and Gun Control Laws.* pg. 2 – 7 3rd Edition Chicago: Chicago University Press, 2010

us our right of protection is no longer necessary, is dangerous to society on two levels. First, the policy not only simply does not work, but in several ways puts the safety of citizens at a greater risk. Second, policies of protection reduce individual empowerment and growth, which leaves *We the People* weak and vulnerable to tyranny.

The studies conducted by Lott, beyond a doubt have demonstrated that the basic progressive supposition, which holds that gun control reduces violence, is factually incorrect. In addition, the data reveals that gun control further exposes weaker individuals to the violent acts of stronger individuals without an effective means of defending themselves. In the public forum, this consideration is largely absent from the debate. On the empirical data, it is worth mentioning that the government – in addition to the media who report on crime at their behest – intentionally skew results in support of the gun control narrative, which in and of itself should be alarming. The media underreports and politicians too frequently ignore the instances when guns were used in acts of defense.[102] In response to the conservative claim that more citizens permitted to carry firearms would logically result in less criminal boldness, the countering progressive narrative is one of fear. And it is all the more disturbing that it is fear of each other that they prey on. However, there is no evidence to suggest that permitting law-abiding citizens to arm themselves for their own responsible protection has ever, or will ever lead to irresponsible gun use and unavoidable violence against other citizens or members of authority:

"The evidence shows that such fears are unfounded: although thirty-one states had so-called nondiscretionary concealed-handgun laws when this book was first written, some of them decades old; there existed only one recorded incident of a permitted, concealed handgun being used in a shooting following a traffic accident, and that involved self-defense. No permit holder has ever shot a police officer, and there have been cases where permit holders have used their guns to save officers' lives."[103]

Although I would like to soon turn attention to the psychological and Natural Law elements to this debate, I would first underscore that even government studies cannot support the anti-2nd Amendment narrative. In Justice Department studies conducted on the 1994 gun ban showing pockets of periods when gun violence decreased, *government* experts believed numerous factors contributed to the drop in these and other crimes; including changing drug markets, a strong economy, better policing and higher incarceration rates. Attempts by progressive politicians to cherry-pick this data have been allowed to propagate flat-out lies, without a single person across the isle citing the government's own experts:

---

[102] Ibid. pg. 12
[103] Ibid. pg. 13

"Attributing the decline in gun murders and shootings to the AW-LCM ban is problematic, however, considering that crimes with LCMs appear to have been steady or rising since the ban...Similarly, neither medical nor criminological data sources have shown any post- ban reduction in the percentage of crime-related gunshot victims who die."[104]

Equally important as the finding by the Justice Department that the ban itself was ineffective, is that the study supports the conservative position that legislation cannot rectify the societal damage from family decomposition. Laws cannot negate the psychological effects of neglecting our growth needs. The correlation between family composition, poverty, education and violence, must be addressed with the assumption that all other efforts are futile unless this cycle is broken. Focusing on mental health rather than the inanimate object as I have claimed throughout this entire discussion is long overdue as it relates to the study of politics. The relationship between progressives and the entertainment industry has long been established, yet it is telling how we focus not on policy to prevent mental illness, but reward the politically connected who aid the progressive narrative – no matter the damage:

"Research has associated exposure to media violence with a variety of physical and mental health problems for children and adolescents, including aggressive and violent behavior, bullying, desensitization to violence, fear, depression, nightmares, and sleep disturbances...Several different psychological and physiologic processes underlie media-violence effects on aggressive attitudes, beliefs, behaviors, and emotions, and these processes are well understood."[105]

Unlike the wealth-producing and mental health-damaging culture of the entertainment industry, providing for one's own security is empowering, and contrary to the progressive narrative it is a source of mental growth. Self-esteem is pursued in many different fashions, and for many Americans, the gun culture has been a source of societal happiness. In truth, this is very much in line with human nature and the state of nature. For instance, every citizen has the right of self-protection. Whether humankind is in a raw state of nature, or entered into a social contract, no force on Earth can deny them self-defense. In the absence of police protection, which at some point will be the case, isn't an absurd assumption to deny citizens the right to defend themselves? However, with such a right, nature has also endowed us with a duty to familiarize ourselves with the adequate means to do so in a responsible fashion. This is what Thomas Jefferson

---

[104] Koper, Christopher S. *An Updated Assessment of the Federal Assault Weapons Ban: Impacts on Gun Markets and Gun Violence, 1994 – 2003*. pg. 92 Report to the National Institute of Justice, United States Department of Justice. University of Pennsylvania: June, 2004
[105] Council on Communications and Media from the American Academy of Pediatric. *Media Violence*. Vol. 124 No. 5 November 1st, 2009

was referring to when he wrote that a citizen "has no natural right in opposition to his social duties."[106] Whether some Americans are disinterested in this responsibility, or simply succumbing to the human weakness to defer that which is hard, the unnatural deference subjects us to exploitations by despots. As reason concludes and history validates, the result is the loss of personal sovereignty, and an emergence of an even greater threat to personal safety than could ever be posed by other citizens – tyranny.

The bias aims to pit citizens against each other, or to make us fear our safety in the presence of other citizens, but ultimately this effort is to misdirect our attention away from the greatest threat to life and liberty – government. In the era of the American Revolution, war was the leading cause of unnatural human death. However, war has since been far surpassed by government in the 20th century as the leading cause, encompassing much of the so-called Progressive Era.[107] It is evident that the shift away from Natural Law, which directs us to fear government, toward the moral imperative to trust in government control is not "progress" at all. Democide, as defined by Russell, is "the murder of any person or people by a government, including genocide, politicide and mass murder; and although the figures are dynamic, six times as many people died as a result of democide during the 20th century than in all that century's wars combined."[108]

While the systems of government and policy approaches to democide vary, there are two commonalities observed in societies that have been subjected to democide. The ruled, which is an appropriate title for Europeans and other peoples are not privy to citizenship as we understand it, have all forfeited the duty of self-defense and other rights of protection. Furthermore, government engages in an assault on civil society with objectives that include the disintegration of the political and social institutions of culture, language, national feelings, religion, and the economic existence of national groups; the destruction of the personal security, liberty, health, dignity; and the lives of the individuals belonging to such groups.[109] The progressive attack on the culture of the Protestant ethic; the demeaning of the importance of the English language; their globalist tendencies hostile to the idea of American exceptionalism; their push for secularism; their economic policies toward black Americans and other national groups; the constant gun control proposals; intolerance of the individual and promotion of indignity through social welfare, all are policies that meet the criteria above – verbatim.

---

[106] Jefferson, Thomas. *The Writing of Thomas Jefferson*. Edited by Albert Ellery Bergh. Vol. 16 pg. 282 Washington D.C.: The Thomas Jefferson Memorial Association, 1907

[107] Davis, Stephen T. *Encountering Evil: Live Options in Theodicy*. Revised Edition. Westminster John Knox Press, 2001

[108] Rummel, R.J. *Death By Government*. New Brunswick, NJ: Transaction Publishers, 1994

[109] Lemkin, Raphael. *Axis Rule in Occupied Europe: Laws of Occupation, Analysis of Government, Proposals for Redress*. Clark, NJ: Lawbook Exchange, 2008 and Ibid.

All of the human tragedies studied by Rummel and others who document democide, have occurred throughout a period that the academic establishment, politicians and media culture, would have us believe was and still is the era of "progress." In total, this era of "progress" and blind trust in government has resulted in 262 million victims of democide; 262 million growth needs never to be fulfilled, of which it is immeasurable to know how each personal journey may have potentially benefited humankind. In the following chapter we will examine the evidence with reason and logic to conclude the following: even though progressives denounce and mock the existence of Natural Law, their actions and objectives suggest that the elites recognize its existence fully; and in reality, it is the manipulation of our human nature as dictated by Natural Law that they contrive to misdirect us away from discovering, or rediscovering.

CHAPTER 4: THE CHOICE

"I hold the maxim no less applicable to public than to private affairs, that honesty is the best policy."[1]

George Washington

HONESTY IS THE BEST POLICY

The debate between conservatism and progressivism, in essence, is a debate between absolute versus relative truth. Progressive ideology, by definition, is diametrically opposed to absolute truth, as the needs of the State are ever-changing – they "progress." Logic, reason, history and measures of empirical evidence, all demonstrate that the result will not match the poll-tested rhetoric. It is only in the absolute truth of Natural Law that we even derive our belief in the equality of life, liberty, and the pursuit of happiness. Government is, and always will be, an oppressive institution that appeals only to the first and second forces of human behavior. Yet, they implement policy that reflects a belief in only the second force, which we have established is the antithesis to our founding principles. Virtue, as defined and understood here is a relic filled with archaic notions that are problematic when forming a more "inclusive society." The ancients Greeks had a name for this arrogant mindset – hubris. Progressives, or all proponents of big government, are either unwilling to except the self-determination of the masses, or unwilling to trust in our capacity for goodness.

Conservatism, on the other hand, is by nature the belief in the preservation of absolute truth. The importance of traditional institutions, such as the family and community, stems from their proven effectiveness to maintain the happiness and well-being of our society. Conservatism is the recognition that it is only in Nature's moral law that we preserve our rights to equality, liberty, and property. True conservatism, in obedience with Natural Law, must never condone the exclusion of our citizens regardless of the changing needs of the State, as it is the belief in the potential of all human beings to be just and good. The belief relies on the observation that America's history has proven the very possibility that people can be just and good, and that is worth conserving. Alexis de Tocqueville, whom I have quoted frequently in this examination as a witness to past American virtue, concluded that America sustained duty to our communities through a reliance on traditional family, religious principles and the universal laws of morality, all of which display humankind's potential to be just and good:

"I sought for the greatness and genius of America in her commodious harbors and her ample

---

[1] *Washington's Farewell Address.* Huszar, George B.; Littlefield, Henry W.; and Littlefield, Arthur W. *Basic American Documents.* Ames, Iowa: Littlefield, Adams & Co. 1953

rivers, and it was not there; in her fertile fields and boundless prairies, and it was not there; in her rich mines and her vast world commerce, and it was not there. Not until I went to the churches of America and heard her pulpits aflame with righteousness did I understand the secret of her genius and power. America is great because she is good, and if America ever ceases to be good, America will cease to be great."[2]

The painful nature of introspection makes it a difficult exercise for the human mind to practice individually, let alone collectively. In the study of any of the social sciences it is a rare to nonexistent phenomena. But we can take solace in the knowledge we share a national identity with a record of breaking the rules of conventional wisdom. In his farewell address Washington said, "I hold the maxim no less applicable to public than to private affairs, that honesty is the best policy."[3] If we were to be honest in our introspection, then it would seem this examination has proven evident the need for all Americans to honestly look in the mirror. Americans who consider themselves ideologically "progressive" must reconcile with themselves the fact that the ideology presupposes a negative view of humanity. The concerns of the progressive ideology are of only the basic primal and psychological needs of human beings, and leave no room for personal growth, nor is it optimistic of our possibility to grow at all. Conservatives, at least the conservatives of our day, must reconcile that we cannot withdraw inward, place an over-emphasis on the individual, and despise others who cannot meet their own basic needs. If in our minds the civic obligation to families, communities, and ourselves is an unduly burden upon our own pursuit of happiness and comfort, then we do for now. Yet, we proceed to democratic despotism with the understanding that the right to one's self-interest has always been contingent upon the happiness of other Americans. Nature will continue to cause us to search for other vehicles to lessen our burdens. For many, government has become that vehicle absent sufficient philanthropic efforts. Our unalienable right to life, liberty, and the pursuit of happiness was not intended to protect the pursuit of selfishness, as others are left to their own misery.

THE NATURE OF GOVERNMENT

If we are to continue with an honest dialogue, then we must dispel these false notions that government can be a means to admirable ends; for which, the government serves as an extension of the greater community of the nation. Inclusiveness, equality, "fairness," and so on, are rhetorical tactics constructed to

---

[2] Quoted from Benson, Ezra Taft. *God, Family, Country: Our Three Great Loyalties.* pg. 360 Salt Lake City: Deseret Book Company, 1975

[3] *Washington's Farewell Address.* Huszar, George B.; Littlefield, Henry W.; and Littlefield, Arthur W. *Basic American Documents.* Ames, Iowa: Littlefield, Adams & Co. 1953

throw the American people off of their odorous scent. Mohandas Gandhi observed:

"Political power, in my opinion, cannot be our ultimate aim. It is one of the means used by men for their all-round advancement. The power to control national life through national representatives is called political power. Representatives will become unnecessary if the national life becomes so perfect as to be self-controlled. It will then be a state of enlightened anarchy in which each person will become his own ruler...In an ideal State there will be no political institution and therefore no political power. That is why Thoreau has said in his classic statement that the government is the best which governs the least."[4]

Government behavior can be likened to that of an oceanic whitetip shark. The species inhabits every region in the world except for the Arctic and Antarctic regions. It has on occasion, much to the surprise of experts, breached territory previously thought to be unacceptable to the creature. The oceanic whitetip is a large, domineering, and opportunistic predator commonly known to follow ships traveling through the open water. They are aggressive and unforgiving in their predation. But to the unsuspecting seafarer the shark, if even noticed, seems no more threatening than a dog trolling their master starving for attention. Unfortunately, it is not attention the oceanic whitetip is starving for. The shark is starving for complacent seafarers who become careless and unthreatened by the dangers posed in the state of nature. They move slow but always deliberate, patiently awaiting a disaster to present their opportunity. Perhaps, the amount of time the shark is made to wait before obtaining his goal is the cause, but it never ends pretty. When the time finally arrives, all of the pent up desire to exude dominance while being forced into submission is released, resulting in a feeding frenzy. Animals, once competitive in ambition, unify to ensure the decimation of the object that Natural Law has deemed to be their prey. Once in the water, the seafarers are helpless to rewind time in hopes of correcting the error of their carelessness.

The nature of government is no different. Attempts to define the boundaries that government is not willing to operate within will prove the attempter ignorant. The body of the State naturally grows to sizes sufficient enough that it makes mounting a challenge difficult, if not foolish. Constant watch and suspicion of their movements is necessary, as not to lose sight of the government's true intentions. Government is but a unity of individuals, with whom, nature has instilled with solitary ambition. Although each individual pursues their own ambition, we must always expect that they are all pursuing the same goal – more power. It may appear to the governed, as the vessel does to the seafarer, that mass numbers provide protection to the individual. This is a false sense of

---

[4] Gandhi, Mohandas, Karamchand. *Enlightened Anarchy*. Selection from "Nations and Identities." Edited by Vincent Pecora. pg. 215 Malden, MA: Blackwell Publishers, 2001

comfort that provides us a reason for complacency. As does the oceanic whitetip, the government will unify to achieve an overwhelming force, which is capable of decimating the opposition to their goal. Much like the feeding frenzy of the sharks, afterwards they will divide the spoils by any means necessary, so long as they've had their desired share.

There is a simple fundamental misunderstanding, even among conservatives, concerning the nature of government and the appropriate role for government in the lives of the American people. Conservatives, for instance, are so consumed with the idea of limited government that they have forgotten limited government is an end, not a means to the preservation of liberty. That is to say, by nature, all government is progressive – even limited government. The antithesis to big government is not limited government, but rather strong civil societies. By managing the limits of big government we are blinded to the measures we can take, which in the end will inevitably render government unnecessary. Big government is born out of the weaknesses within civil society. If we strengthen our civil society, then the liberty opposing forces of government will be crushed under the weight of that massive body of territory that separates the individual citizen from the State – the community. In the tightness of our relationships, within our individual communities, is from where the freedom wielding Sword of Damocles will come to fall upon tyrants.

CONCLUSION

Approaching the study of politics from a diversity of disciplines in order to construct a worldview that is true to the truth, has long been ignored by academia. Thus, what we know to be true from our real world common sense, or "self-evident" observations is not reflected in the academic literature. The reasons we have previously discussed, but the implication we must literally live with within ourselves, and teach to those who surround us. Building on the inadequate literature will necessarily take time, but in our lives we can move forward to the betterment of humankind by simply adjusting social and political norms, such as the ones constructed by the cage of political correctness. The existence of common sense is in and of itself an observation of a Natural Law, yet we do not even acknowledge it because of the fear of these societal barriers. This is not how a free society conducts a dialogue. The truth is paramount and takes precedent over the sensibilities of a few for the well-being of the whole.

The benefit of religious observation, for instance, seems to be a common sense conclusion. Yet it is widely ignored, or even consciously buried. The vast majority of the post-Bill of Rights amendments were designed to concentrate power, but the idea of rolling back government is portrayed as ridiculous. The 17th Amendment, specifically, is celebrated as a victory for "fairness" and democratic principle, but it is enslaving us. We should be readily willing to admit to ourselves that the grim results outweigh the ideological benefits, as they are not a benefit to us at all. But until we understand that beneath these structural-based solutions is a deeper problem of values, we will never render government unnecessary and improper.

The choice is clear. The evidence from American history, specifically regarding the Progressive Movement, is that Americans not surprisingly follow the same pattern of Natural Law that was observed by our Founding Fathers almost 300 years ago. What could be considered a surprise for some is that despite the rhetoric tailored to sound like "progress," the progressive ideology is in reality, truly regressive. Conservative principles seek to protect what we as students of our own history and nature know to be true, but this does not carry within it a stigma of backwardness. Our Founders believed very much in the idea of progress, however, simply because an ideology is given such a term it does not follow that the ideology is true to its meaning in practice. The principles of our founding documents surviving through the success of American Revolution were a collection of observations in absolute truths. The vast majority of the post-Bill of Rights amendments to the Constitution were the end result of efforts to concentrate power and grow government. Of course, this suggests that although "progressive" leaders scoff at the universal tenets of Natural Law, they are completely aware of its existence and have been manipulating our nature in accordance with it.

The feeling we as Americans are experiencing, a feeling that something is just not right with the time, which we feel in our collective stomach and heart, is a result of our government's decision to abandon our national identity. There has, indeed, occurred "a long train of abuses and usurpations." They are forcing our society to "progress" against the grain of Natural Law. Naturally, we are feeling this force, as our Creator has instilled in us an innate instinct, or a biological alarm if you will, which alerts us to danger and threats to our happiness. Do not hit the snooze button on this alarm, as it is time to once again wake up and provide for our "future security."

As Americans, we are blessed to have inherited such a unique national identity, which is one who fully understands the potential of free, autonomous people. However, we too have inherited an enormous responsibility, which is far more important in practice than in rhetorical gesture. When we are good to each other we grow together, and we do so at the benefit of all humankind. It is for this reason above all; that as liberty loving people we cannot ignore or defer our civic obligations if we hope to retain what little freedom remains today. Until we come to rebuild liberty's civil defenses, the cycle of exploitation will continue. Progressive policies are tailored to appeal to our fears and needs, both of which are ever-lasting elements to human nature, which is why despots have returned to the same practices throughout human civilization. However, in government's efforts to satisfy only our basic needs, and in our efforts to shrink away from our obligation to fulfill them, our growth needs are abandoned or ignored, or both. As a result, individuals cannot grow within themselves to the tallest heights of human potential, and as an extension society and the nation cannot grow. The prospect of a bright future for future generations is bleak, and even bleaker will it be if we continue to refuse our obligation to our Creator to care for our fellow-citizens. This was not always the case in America, nor does it have to be in the future; but without a course correction the virtue of the human Spirit and connection will diminish, and our goodness and obligation will soon vanish along with them. That is the real world result and most frightening promise of big government. It holds the making of an unhealthy society ripe for despotism, a collection of self-centered individuals unworthy of what Samuels Adams called the "gift of Heaven," not a virtuous republic.

ABOUT THE AUTHOR

Richard D. Baris is the Creator and Senior Editor at the PeoplesPunditDaily.com. He is also a popular political columnist and blogger, who has been a journalist, entrepreneur, political speaker and academic. Rich is a veteran of the U.S. Army, who studied Political Science, International Relations, and History at the University of Florida.

www.ingramcontent.com/pod-product-compliance
Lightning Source LLC
Chambersburg PA
CBHW060149300526
45790CB00014B/389